A Friend's Love Will Overcome:

A COLLECTION OF TEACHINGS, POEMS AND SONGS

BRIAN HOLLOP

Table *of* Contents

A Friend's Love Will Overcome:

A Collection of Teachings, Poems and Songs

BRIAN HOLLOP

INK START MEDIA
265 Eastchester Dr Ste 133 #102
High Point NC 27262

Jesus said unto him, Thou shalt love the Lord thy God with all thy heart,
and with all thy soul, and with all thy mind.
This is the first and great commandment.
And the second is like unto it, Thou shalt love thy neighbor as thyself.
On these two commandments hang all the law and the prophets.
(Matt. 22: (37-40))

Acknowledgements

I would like to thank the following:

God the Father for creating me and having a plan for my life.

God the Son, Jesus Christ, for dying on the Cross for my sins.

The Holy Spirit for being there to comfort and protect me through the hard times.

My parents for raising me to be a godly man and caring for me.

My sister for being nice to me growing up.

My brother-in-law for being nice to my sister.

My two nieces for their inspiration and determination.

My nephew who has the wisdom of Solomon.

The rest of my beautiful family and friends. &

    The reader for taking the time to read this book.

About the Author

I was born at Lawrence Hospital in Bronxville, New York on November 26, 1978. At the time, my parents were living in Yonkers, New York. In 1980, my family moved to Wappingers Falls, New York.

From September 1984 to June 1986, I went to Kinry Road Elementary School in Poughkeepsie, New York for kindergarten and first grade. I was declared mentally retarded by doctors and put in special needs classes. It was during this time in my life that my mom was saved and the Lord healed my mind.

I went to Vassar Road Elementary School in Poughkeepsie, New York for second, third, and fourth grade. I was still in special needs classes; however, I began to excel in my studies.

For fifth grade, I went to a private school called Upton Lake Christian Academy in Clinton Corners, New York. At this school I was no longer placed in special needs classes.

From sixth to eighth grade, I went to a private school in Poughkeepsie, New York from September 1990 to June 1993. It was during this time that the Lord showed me the difference between being religious and having a personal relationship with the Lord. The Lord also showed me the dangers of gossip and legalism.

From September 1993 to June 1997, I went to Roy C. Ketcham High School from grades nine through twelve. I was on the honor- roll. It was during this time that I got my first job working at Kmart on April 22nd, 1996.

After high school, I went to Dutchess Community College from August 1997 to December 1999. My first choice for a major in college was engineering. After the third semester, I changed my major to accounting. I got my associates degree in business administration in December 1999.

After my time at Dutchess Community College, I transferred my credits to the State University of New York (SUNY) at New Paltz so that I could get my bachelor of science (BS) degree in accounting. I went to SUNY at New Paltz from January 2000 to December 2001. I was on the Dean's List.

After I got my BS degree in accounting, I continued part-time at SUNY at New Paltz for my MBA in accounting from January 2002 to December 2006. While I was studying for my MBA at SUNY New Paltz, the Lord blessed me with a couple of different work positions. I continued working at Kmart until June 2004. I worked as a temp accounting clerk at a marketing firm called The Listworks Corporation from June 2004 to January 2005. This was my first job in the accounting field. After the Listworks Corporation, I worked as a temp at a pharmaceutical company called Boehringer-Ingelheim as an accounts payable processor from March 2005 to October 2005. Shortly after my position at Boehringer-Ingelheim ended, I got a position as a temp for General Electric (GE) in their personal property tax department as an accounting analyst. I worked in this position from November 2005 to October 2006. When the position at GE was over, I got a full-time permanent position at an accounting firm in Purchase, New York in November 2006. I am still working for this company.

I am currently living in Wappingers Falls, New York and continue to see the Lord's hand in my life as I seek Him for guidance and direction.

Introduction

A friend loveth at all times, and a brother is born for adversity, (Prov. 17:17)

This book is about lessons the Lord has taught me over the years and about His love in my life. The Lord has healed me and His love has helped me to overcome many challenges. I only hope that this book will help the reader understand the love that God has for him or her.

What Do You Think?

There are seven reasons this book was written.

One major reason this book was written was to give thanks to the Lord for who He is and for the people that He has blessed me with. Your relationship with the Lord should be the most important in your life. The second most important relationship is with family. Finally, you should thank the Lord for your friends and other people He has brought into your life. What good is a job or anything else without the Lord and the people He has blessed you with?

The second reason this book was written is in testimony of the great things the Lord has done in my life. Before the Lord came into my life, doctors and teachers declared me mentally retarded. The Lord has brought me a long way. He changed me from a boy with no future to a man who has lots of family and friends, an MBA in accounting, an excellent job as a tax accountant, and a chance to be with Him for all eternity. It does not matter what people say about you. Only what the Lord says matters. These testimonies will be in the sections on **Life Experience**. We will go into the different sections within each lesson shortly.

The third reason for this book is to get people to confess their sins and turn back to Him. Sin separates us from God's love. By confessing sin to the Lord, we are able to better understand His plan for our lives. This is easier said than done. A lot of times we confess things to the Lord but go right back into those sins. We cannot overcome sin by ourselves, but only through the Lord who strengthens us. Only by allowing the Lord to help us resist the temptations of sin are we going to succeed.

The fourth reason this book was written is to let people know that the Lord is the same great, mighty, good, and personal Lord today as He was in biblical times. Things change whether we like it or not. With things changing around us all the time it can be hard to remember that He is with us. Thankfully, the Lord, His commandments, and His love for us never change.

The fifth reason this book was written is to address some of the most deadly sins crippling the body of Christ today. These sins include materialism, gossip, lust, covetousness, legalism, and unforgiveness. What makes these sins so deadly is that the churches in this land are not aware of them. By becoming aware of them, I pray that churches will pray to be delivered so that they can hear clearly from the Lord. The Lord desires to speak to and hear from His people.

The sixth reason this book was written is to draw people back to His plan and direction for their lives. The Lord has a plan for everybody. His plans are designed to help us grow and not to harm us. The Lord wants us to appreciate the gifts He has given us. He does not want us to settle for second-rate plans for our lives.

The final reason this book was written is to get people ready for when the Lord returns. The Lord is coming back to a glorious church. However, how can we be that glorious church when we are still walking around in sin, fear, and defeat? We are children of the Lord. We will be ruling and reigning with Him. Do not settle for things in this life because earth is not our home. Our home is with Him and His love for all eternity.

Challenge:

This book is not like any other Christian book I have ever seen. The problem with a lot of Christian books today is that they are too long, boring, religious, and difficult to understand.

In this book, poems, songs, skits, and life experiences are used in each lesson to make learning about the Lord more enjoyable. With this book, I hope the reader will not just experience another religious belief or formula, but will develop a personal relationship with the Lord. There are also challenges at the end of every chapter that will help the reader in their personal walk with Christ.

Each chapter starts with a Bible verse. After the verse, there is an opening to the next section. The sections could be titled **Poem/Song, Life Experience,** or **What Do You Think.**

The **Poem/Song** section shows a collection of poems or songs that the Lord has given me over the years. Some of the poems in this section may have choruses to sing. The parts that are to be sung are in bold. Other poems can be used as skits to be acted out in churches, parks, etc.

The **Life Experience** section shows my testimony and what the Lord was showing me through different times in my life. As mentioned earlier, I was declared mentally retarded with no hope of a future. One will see in these sections how the Lord transformed me from someone having no hope to someone having a great God, a wonderful family, an MBA in accounting, and a permanent job.

The **What Do You Think** section is about the lessons the Lord has shown me about Him and about life. This section also contains things I have pondered over the years. As you read these sections, feel free to agree and disagree as you see fit.

Not all lessons will have a **Poem/Song** section. Some lessons will not have a **What Do You Think** section while others will not have a **Life Experience** section.

Every lesson ends with a **Challenge**. The **Challenge** section concludes the lesson and also contains an exercise the reader can do to apply what was being taught in the lesson.

Studying a book about the Lord may sound great. However, we cannot do it all by ourselves. We fall short of the glory of God. Jesus is the only way, truth, and life. Only through His love are we able to overcome our circumstances and have everlasting life.

Please take some time to skim through the book to see how the different sections within the lessons are listed. As you do so, ask yourself, if you could write a book about the Lord, what would you call it?

This is My commandment,

That ye love one another, as I have loved you.

Greater love hath no man than this,

that a man lay down his life for his friends.

Ye are my friends,

if ye do whatsoever I command you.

Henceforth I call you not servants;

for the servant knoweth not what his lord doeth: but I have called you friends; for all things that I have heard of my Father I have made known unto you.

Ye have not chosen me,

but I have chosen you, and ordained you, that ye should go and bring forth fruit, and that your fruit should remain: that whatsoever ye shall ask of the Father in my name, he may give it you.

(John 15: 12-16)

LESSON 1
Higher than Anything

"For thus saith the high and lofty One that inhabiteth eternity, whose name is Holy; I dwell in the high and holy place, with him also that is of a contrite and humble spirit, to revive the spirit of the humble, and to revive the heart of the contrite ones." (Isai. 57: 15)

God is all powerful, all mighty, and all knowing. Sometimes we are guilty of limiting God. We like to take God and put Him in our own little boxes. We have our own image of how God should look and what He can do and what he can't do.

This first poem is to remind us that all things are possible with God. He can do anything. He can use anyone and anything to give Himself the glory. He is greater than anything we can imagine.

Poem/Song

Our God is Out of the Box
Our God is out of the box.
He is Lord of all the Seas & docks
He will build up your life like lego blocks.
Because our God is out of the box.

Chorus

Our God is out of the box
Remove from him those chains and locks.
Don't control him like robots
Stop pointing to those clocks.
Because our God is out of the box.
Our God is out of the box
He is stronger than an ox.
He is smarter than a fox.
He'll protect you better than Fort Knox.
He can heal cancer, aids, and small pox.
Because our God is out of the box.

Chorus

Our God is Out of the Box
He can provide greater than any bonds or stocks.
He is mightier than any flocks.
He always knows how it rocks.
He hits more homers than the Yankees and Red Sox.
Because our God is out of the box.

Chorus

Please let him on out of that box.
Don't keep him inside your lines and dots.
Stop limiting him with your chains and locks.
Because our God is out of the Box.

What Do You Think?

He is higher than the mountains. He is higher than the buildings. He is higher than the clouds. He is higher than the sky. He is higher than the sun, moon, and stars.

God has no opposites. No force is powerful enough to fight Him. No foe is worthy to even challenge Him.

The Lord created everything. His beauty can be seen in His creation all around us.

The devil is nothing compared to God. The devil surely is defeated from that first day he got prideful and got thrown out of heaven.

We have absolutely nothing to fear. Do not be distressed when there is talk of economic recession, wars, and rumors of wars.

He can stop a war with one word. He can deliver us with one prayer.

Where is your faith, you children of the King of Kings and the Lord of Lords? You just need faith the size of a mustard seed and you will see Him deliver you from the snares and cares of this world. Remember, a mustard tree grows from the tiniest of seeds to the largest of trees. So will His hand be with us if we nurture and grow what He has given us in our lives.

Challenge

What can men or demons do to us? Fear the one who can kill both the body and the soul. Fear the Lord and you will have the courage to deal with anything. Anything else is nothing to God. Are there things that you are putting above the Lord? Use this time right now to think about some things that you are currently worrying about and ask the Lord to strengthen your faith in these areas.

LESSON 2

The All-Knowing God

"Known unto God are all his works from the beginning of the world."
(Acts 15:8)

We have so much to be thankful for. He provides us with plenty of food and shelter. He provides us with clothing. He provides for the birds and flowers. How much more precious is a person?

Sometimes we take all that He has done for us for granted. We use His death on the cross as an excuse to keep sinning.

Sometimes we are not satisfied with what we have and want more. We want a new car or a new house just because someone else got a new one.

This next poem is about giving the Lord thanks for everything you have.

Poem/Song:

It's Not About the Turkey
You don't have to graduate with a PHD from Berkley
To know that Thanksgiving is not just about the turkey.
Thanksgiving is about what the Lord has done.
Thank the Lord for all that's fun.
Thank you for this joyous time.
Thank the Lord with this rhyme.

Chorus

**Rub a dub dub,
thanks for the grub.
Gobble gobble
makes the mind boggle.
Is that all we have to be thankful for?
I thank the Lord for providing more.**
Thank the Lord for dying on the cross.

Thank Him for being the boss.
I thank Him that He is God.
Whether I eat turkey or cod.
Remember as you fill your bellies and tanks.
Today is not about the turkey but thanks.
Thank you for this joyous time.
Thank the Lord with this rhyme.

Chorus

As you dress up so nice and perky.
Give thanks when you enjoy that turkey.
Thank Him for your health.
Thank Him for your wealth.
Do not sit in denial and pride.
Humble yourself while you search inside.
We would have nothing but our sin.
If we did not have blessings from Him.
Thank you for this joyous time.
Thank the Lord with this rhyme.

Chorus

Don't be jerky
when you eat that turkey.
Thank Him for your lover.
Thank the Lord for His cover.
Thank Him for his strong hand.
Thank Him for being with you to stand.
For your family and friends be humble.
Give thanks or you will stumble.
Be thankful for your blessings.
Or else all you will have is turkey dressings.
Thank you for this joyous time.
Thank the Lord with this rhyme.

Chorus

What Do You Think?

The Lord is all-knowing. I know nothing compared to His wisdom. I pray that I will be in His will. I ask Him for answers to the major things as well as the minor. All the decisions we make are important to Him.

I need the Lord to give me the strength to act on His words. The years ahead are going to be tough. However, with the Lord on my side, why should I be afraid?

I know only a little about life. One thing I do know is that the Lord loves me. I also know that the Lord always answers prayer. I know that if the Lord is for us, who can be against us? In time, the Lord will give me just the answer I need so that I cannot deny it is from Him.

Forgive me, Lord, for my foolishness and for my lack of faith. Build up my faith, Lord. I cannot imagine one day without knowing that Jesus loves me. I also can't imagine a day without knowing that He is watching over me. I need to be reminded sometimes that He is good and judges us righteously.

Challenge

Wisdom does not always come from a book. It comes from the experiences we have in our everyday lives. Other people are also important in our learning.

The Bible says that the fear of the Lord is the beginning of wisdom. Fearing the Lord means that we need to give the Lord reverence. A great way to show the Lord reverence is to give Him thanks for what He has given you. Thank Him for a place to live. Thank Him for food to eat. Thank Him for a job, Thank Him for your health. Take this time to make a list of things to be thankful for and praise Him for your blessings.

LESSON 3
Thank You for My Family and Friends

"Wherefore come out from among them, and be ye separate, saith the Lord, and touch not the unclean thing; and I will receive you, And will be a Father unto you, and ye shall be my sons and daughters, saith the Lord Almighty."
(2 Cori. 6: 17-18)

We have a personal God. To God the Father, we are His children. To Jesus Christ, we are His brothers and sisters.

Our sins kept us from knowing and loving God. In order to remove the barrier that our sins have created, God the Father sent Jesus Christ into the world to die for our sins.

In this next poem, one will see the love that Jesus had for us and what He suffered so that we can be with Him as a family for all of eternity.

Poem/Song

Bad Day
If you think you had a bad day.
Remember the price He had to pay.
Bom Bom Bom Bom Bom Bom Bom Bom
Bum Bum Bum
Bum Bum Bum Bum
Oh Oh Oh Boy!!
So you feel down on your luck.
And your day is like yuck.
Your day may be tough.
But Jesus had it rough.
He gave away His glory and powers.
to suffer all of those hours.
He died up on that cross.
Just to keep us from gettin lost.
So He came off of his throne.
To come down to our zone.
So you don't know what to do.
Remember He suffered all this for you.

Chorus

So you think you had a bad day.
But think of the price He had pay.
He gave all his glory and power away.
To suffer all that pain and dismay.
To provide all of us with a way.
So we can be with Him someday
Hey Hey.
Bom Bom Bom Bom Bom Bom Bom Bom
Bum Bum Bum
Bum Bum Bum Bum
Oh Oh Oh Boy!!
So you think your day is a mess?
And you're not functioning at best.
Jesus was born in a manger.
To suffer through all of life's danger.
He had to sleep on the hay.
Mary and Joseph He had to obey.
He gave up where He had more than enough,
To suffer for us all through this stuff.
He had to travel around and drift
Because people wanted to throw Him off of a cliff.
He died for us because He is merciful and meek,
Even though we treat it all like He was weak.
So you don't know what to do?
Remember, He suffered all this for you.

Chorus

So you think life is unfair?
And it seems like no one would care.
Remember how He was falsely accused.
Jesus was beaten and abused.
He was betrayed by Judas with a kiss.
That was not a lot of bliss.
His disciples turned and fled.
They forsook Him as dead.
You think all of this was nice?
Peter denied Him before the cock crowed thrice.
Even though Jesus was fully equipped,
He chose to be beaten and whipped.
So you don't know what to do?
Remember, He suffered all this for you.

Chorus

So you think you're in pain?
Jesus took on Him all of your shame.
He was led up before Pilate.
He was treated worse than a pirate.
He had to lug that cross through the street.
As the soldiers mocked and beat.
All the way to Golgotha, the place of the skull,
The Lord had to suffer a lot of bull.
And those soldiers that were varmints
Cast lots for His garments.
So you don't know what to do?
Remember, He suffered all this for you.

Chorus

So nothing good you can detect?
Remember the Lord, who gets no respect.
After all He did, people still feel ashamed
To say they believe on Jesus' name.
People still call Him a louse.
And they defile His house.
The love of His people He desires to seek.
He is lucky to see us an hour a week.
With our issues we are still on His top ten.
If He had to, He would go through that day again.
Remember on the cross what was done.
Remember, Jesus Christ is God's Son.
He died for every girl and boy.
So that we can all shout for Joy.
So you don't know what to do?
Remember, He suffered all this for you.

Chorus

What Do You Think?

Life is precious to the Lord. The life you live is precious to the Lord.

How we live our lives on earth determines where we will be for all eternity. We meet people for a season and then they are gone. Every person has an impact on another person.

Why is it that there are days when you just wake up, eat breakfast, and go to work as if everything is all right, but on other days, you need to pray for help just to get out of bed in the morning? Sometimes you get this feeling even when there is nothing wrong in your life.

I thank You, Lord, for the time with my parents. Lots of people grow up with only one parent or no parents at all.

I thank You, Lord, for a great mother who loved me enough to teach me about the love of Jesus. I thank the Lord that I have a mother who fears the Lord more than man.

I thank You, Lord, for blessing me with a great father who understands things and who shows great compassion for people.

I will cherish the time I spend with them. Words cannot describe my love for them.

Can I pay the amount their correction was worth? Can I buy another minute with my parents?

I thank You, Lord, that I had parents to seek wisdom from. I thank You, Lord, for the godly wisdom You have shown me through them.

I just hope that I can remember everything my parents have shown me when they pass away or when I have my own family to provide for. I hope to be a beacon of light for Jesus and to reach people close to me for the Lord.

I thank You, Lord, for my sister. I thank You, Lord, that we did not fight with each other all the time when we were young. I thank You, Lord, that my sister was there to help me with my problems when I was growing up. I thank You, Lord, that we still get along even today.

I thank You, Lord, for my brother-in-law, who is a loving husband and cares for my sister and their kids. I thank You, Lord, that my sister didn't marry someone who beats her and the kids.

I thank You, Lord, for my older niece. She has so much talent and has the greatest personality.

I thank You, Lord, for my younger niece and for her loving spirit. Manifest Your power through her.

I thank You, Lord, for my nephew. I thank You, Lord, for giving him wisdom like Solomon had in his days.

Please continue to bless and heal my sister and her family. Help them to understand Your faithfulness and goodness.

I am thankful for all my friends when I was growing up. When you lose money, it can be replaced. When you lose friends, they are irreplaceable. Through all the friends I have met throughout my life, I have seen the Lord's love and kindness time and time again. A friend's love cannot be taught or mimicked.

Challenge

Never forget what the Lord gives you. Cherish your friends and praise God for them. Remember that where two or more are gathered in His name, the Lord will be in the midst of them. Think about all the people in your life. Thank the Lord for them and pray that they will come to know the Lord deeper and that the plans of the Devil over their lives will fail. Remember, He that is in you is greater than He that is in the world.

In the beginning was the Word,

and the Word was with God, and the Word was God.

The same was in the beginning with God. All things were made by Him;

and without Him was not any thing made that was made.

In Him was life;

and the life was the light of men.

And the light shineth in darkness;

and the darkness comprehended it not.

(John 1: 1-5)

LESSON 4

The Healing of the Demon Possessed Man

"The Spirit of the Lord is upon me, because He hath anointed me to preach the gospel to the poor; he hath sent me to heal the brokenhearted, to preach deliverance to the captives, and recovering of sight to the blind, to set at liberty them that are bruised, To preach the acceptable year of the Lord."
(Luke 4:18- 19)

In Luke 8: 26-39, Jesus heals a demon-possessed man who had a legion of demons in him. Jesus cast the demons out of the man and into a herd of pigs. The pigs jumped off a cliff and drowned in the water below.

A lot of people would look at this story and say this is the end of the story. For the man who was delivered from demons, I think this was only the beginning.

This story in Luke Chapter 8 is so similar to my life. I thank the Lord that He was with me throughout my whole life and that He never gave up on me.

Life Experience

The devil's plan was for me to be mentally retarded and not able to think for myself. He wanted me to think I was worthless, useless, and a burden to others. The devil, as well as the Lord, has plans for each of our lives.

I don't recall much before the Lord healed my mind. All I know is that I liked to play with building blocks. I failed kindergarten. At the time, my dad was a heavy drinker who would drink a whole twelve pack of beer a day by himself. My mom was very fearful of death because she knew that if she had died back then, she would have gone to hell.

My testimony starts with my mom accepting Jesus into her heart. My mom used to work as a security guard at Indian Point, a power plant in Westchester County, New York. One night, she cried out to Jesus, "Lord if you are real, help me!" The Lord did answer her prayer that night. He sent two men to minister to her. My mom got saved that night. I thank the Lord for the faithfulness of those men, and that they were not afraid to talk to my mom that night.

Mom started reading the Bible. She began praying for me. She refused to believe what the doctors and everyone said about me.

I thank the Lord that my parents did not choose to abort me despite what the doctors said about me. Doctors don't always know all the answers. They can be wrong sometimes.

I remember her reading the Bible one night when a verse stood out to me. It's funny. I can't even recall what the verse said, but it changed my whole life.

I started learning like a sponge. The teachers called my mom and asked her what had happened. Mom told them, "The Lord is healing my son's brain."

I was lucky the Lord gave me such devoted parents, who stood in the gap and prayed for me. I am glad they did not just give up on me when the world told them "No." That year, I made up kindergarten and the first grade.

Whenever anyone asks me if my life was easier or harder after I knew Jesus, I have to say easier. This is because I can't imagine what one day would be like not knowing He is there with me. I would rather wake up knowing that it is the Lord and me versus the world instead of just me versus the world.

When you accept Jesus into your heart, it is no longer just you versus the world. It is Jesus and you versus the world. This frame of mind makes life so much easier when you are being ridiculed and going through your day to day trials.

What Do You Think?

I find it interesting that when the man in Luke 8 asked to follow Jesus, Jesus told him to go back to his own house and testify about the great things God had done for him. This is the only account in the Bible where Jesus actually refuses when someone asked to follow Him.

I'm sure people avoided the man who was delivered from the demons when they saw him in the marketplace. Some people probably still treated him poorly because they still thought of him as being demon-possessed.

This is what happened in my life when the Lord healed me. Before the Lord healed me, I was declared mentally retarded. Even after my healing, people still treated me as if I were retarded. They still discriminated against me. They still told me that I was useless. I thank the Lord that it matters what He says and not what people say.

I wonder if the man who was healed from the legion of demons remained
faithful to Jesus, or did he fall back into sin?

Challenge

Return to thine own house, and shew how great things God hath done unto thee.
And he went his way, and published throughout the whole city how great things
Jesus had done unto him. (Luke 8: 39)

Read the story in Luke 8: 26-39. As you read this passage, think back to when you first accepted the Lord into your life. Think about why you decided to follow the Lord.

Maybe some reading this book are still questioning the Lord and they are still debating whether to accept Jesus into their hearts. If this is you, take some time to think about what you like and don't like about God and meditate on it. Ask the Lord to reveal Himself to you.

LESSON 5
What you Can Do

"Wherefore also we pray always for you, that our God would count you worthy of this calling, and fulfill all the good pleasure of his goodness, and the work of faith with power. That the name of our Lord Jesus Christ may be glorified in you, and ye in him, according to the grace of our God and the Lord Jesus Christ." (2 Thes. 1: 11- 12)

Sometimes we wonder if we are any use to the Lord. The Devil tries to tell us things such as we are no good, that we are not smart enough to proclaim the Lord's name, or that we are an embarrassment to Him.

Remember that Jesus loves you. Remember also that the enemy fears you and will do anything to stop you from serving the Lord. If the Lord puts something on your heart to do, you need to obey the Lord and do it.

As you read this next poem, start thinking about your own talents and skills that you can use to glorify the Lord.

Poem/Song

What's Up
When the Devil asks "Who are you?"
You can say that in Christ this is what I can do.
In the choir I can sing.
Or if someone's down, I can give them a ring.
I can give ministries cash.
I can pick up the trash.
You can be a witness for the Lord.
There is so much you can do to show He's adored.
There is something you can sing when it comes up.
When someone asks you "What's Up"

Chorus

There's the ceiling and the sky.
And the Most High.
When you're down, turn up.
There's the moon and the sun.
And the Holy One.
Sing praise and give it up.
There's the stars in space.
And the Holy Place.
when you're down, look up.
There's one more thing that is up above.
It's the Holy God and His love.
Now everybody give it up.
Now that you know What's up!!!
When the Devil tells you that you're not smart.
Remember Jesus Christ is in your heart.
The Devil says this to discourage you.
But there is so much you can do.
You can hand out Bible tracts on Halloween.
Or during Christmas put out that manger scene.
You can visit people when their sick.
Or show a Christian DVD with just one click.
There is something you can sing when it comes up.
When someone asks you "What's Up"

Chorus

The Devil may tell you that you're no one.
But you can do so much when you have God's Son.
You can send someone a Valentine's card.
Or you can work at your job very hard.
You can shout about the Lord all over the town.
Or teach Bible stories to kids as Bozo the Clown.
You can have a Bible verse on a birthday cake.
Or baptize people in the lake.
There is something you can sing when it comes up.
When someone asks you "What's Up"

Chorus

The Devil may tell you that you will mess up.
Don't listen to the Devil, instead look up.
The Lord is calling and He's proud of you.
You have so many talents and skills that you can do.
You can talk about Jesus in the diner with tea.

You can play worship music on the street for free.
You can help those that are poor.
By buying them food at the store.
There is something you can sing when it comes up.
When someone asks you "What's Up"

Chorus

The Devil will try to give you fear.
Tell the Devil in Jesus name get out of here.
The Devil will say things that aren't true.
But don't let this discourage you.
You can lead a Bible study
Or you can pray with a buddy.
You can study His Book
Or for the church you can cook.
There is something you can sing when it comes up.
When someone asks you "What's Up"

Chorus

Now that you know What's up!!!
When you're down, turn up.
Sing praise and give it up.
when you're down, look up.
Now everybody give it up.
Now that you know What's up!!!
Now that you know
What's up!!!

Life Experience

Even though the Lord healed my mind, for a while the world still treated me as it always had. I was still picked on and made fun of. People still screamed, "Retard!" as I walked down the street.

The Lord may have healed me, but I was not a genius. I still had to go to school to learn.

I think the Lord healed me by giving me the strength and the determination to focus on my studies. I saw my schoolwork as an escape. I felt like no one would let me do anything but schoolwork. I felt like all I could do was wake up, eat, go to school, do my homework, watch TV, and go to bed.

We have to focus on what we can do for the Lord and not on what we can't do. Give the Lord the things you can't do and He will give you the things you *will* do.

Challenge

We may not all preach in a church or be able to quote the whole Bible, but the Lord is just looking for people who will step out and serve Him no matter what their shortcomings are. The Lord uses the weak things to confound the wise. He has a plan and purpose for each person's life.

Think of the talents and the skills the Lord has given you. Use this time now to think of ways that you can give the Lord glory. Make a list of them and pray to the Lord for direction. Even if an idea sounds strange, write it down. Who knows? The Lord may use you to start a new ministry altogether. Remember that our God is out of the box.

This then is the message which we have heard of him,

and declare unto you, that God is light, and in Him is no darkness at all.

If we say that we have fellowship with Him,

and walk in darkness, we lie, and do not the truth:

But if we walk in the light,

as He is in the light, we have fellowship one with another, and the blood of Jesus Christ His Son cleanseth us from all sin.

If we say that we have no sin,

we deceive ourselves, and the truth is not in us.

If we confess our sins,

He is faithful and just to forgive us our sins, and to cleanse us from all unrighteousness.

If we say that we have not sinned,

we make Him a liar, and His Word is not in us.

(I John 1: 5-10)

LESSON 6

The Simpsons without Eyes

"The Lord openeth the eyes of the blind: the Lord raiseth them that are
bowed down: the Lord loveth the righteous:"
(Psal. 146: 8)

Lust is a very destructive sin. It breaks up marriages. It robs one's soul. It favors the outward appearance instead of the inward personality.

Lust is also one of those silent killers. What I mean is that this is a sin that is so accepted in the world today that people don't even recognize it. Lust is used in all sorts of advertising. Lust is in all sorts of entertainment such as books, movies, and even cartoons.

People do not understand how deadly it is. They see this sin as being only as bad as a little white lie.

The truth is that sin is still sin to the Lord whether it is a white lie or murder. All sin must be repented of in order for the Lord to heal us. This poem was written to show how lust infiltrates our lives and how to take a stand against it.

Poem/Song

Porn No
Lust is not love.
Love is not lust.
Love comes from above.
Lust turns to dust.
Lust always tries to capture your eye.
You get instant happiness, then it leaves you dry.
True love has no hidden agenda.
Love is sweet like sugar or Splenda.
When you see men & women nude on the beach,
Lust will shout that this is freedom of speech.
Lust doesn't set you free, it just keeps you bound.
It leaves you empty. So you keep looking around.

Love does not bring deceit and shame.
Love is never quick to blame.
Along with love come peace, goodness, and joys.
It is more than naked people and sex toys.
Lust brings adultery, jealousy, and strife.
Lust never promotes unity between husband and wife.
Love is precious like a diamond or pearl.
Lust just looks at the material world.
Lust looks at the flesh, love looks at so much more.
Along with your body, your spirit love will restore.
Love will build up your mind, body, spirit and soul.
Lust just looks for it's next victim to pull.
Lust looks to take. Love looks to give.
With lust you die. With love you live.
Beware all, lust is on the prowl.
Lust doesn't play games. It's deceitful and foul.
Lust will always say it doesn't hurt to look.
It will promote an ad on TV or in a book.
It will give the impression that it cares
By showing men and women in their underwear.
Lust will work through movies and shows.
Lust robs your dough and ties you up in bows.
It will make sexual sin look like a joke.
It is all a bunch of mirrors and smoke.
Say yes to love and no to porn.
To this thing that keeps the nations torn.
Boycott anything that makes lust seem good.
where you think, "I can sleep with anyone if I could."
A condom doesn't take the place of respect.
It is love that we are called to represent.
If you love them enough, you will say "I do."
When something promotes lust, give it a boo.
The churches need to take a stand.
The world has tried to keep love fanned.
Love will triumph over all.
It can withstand the blast of any fireball.
Lust itself will one day be as dust.
Love will forever be given to us from above.
Always pray to walk in the Lord's Spirit.
Resist flesh, close your eyes and don't hear it.

What Do You Think?

One night, I had a very disturbing dream. In my dream, I saw the characters from "The Simpsons" without their eyes drawn in. The Lord then revealed to me that this is the church. We are spiritually blind and deaf to His words.

Sometimes we see and hear things that keep us from hearing from the Lord. We become spiritually blind and deaf.

What kind of example for Christ can we be for this blind generation if we ourselves are blinded by our sins? We watch pornography, adult comedians, and dirty cartoons that continually take God's name in vain.

I'm not saying that "The Simpsons" is all bad, but I don't think I can watch the show the same way after what the Lord has shown me. The Lord wants us to watch and listen to things that are pure, innocent, and right. He wants us to see clearly.

Don't be unsympathetic when you see another massacre on the news. Don't watch scary movies if they rob your faith in the Lord and replace his Holy Spirit with fear and doubt. Don't watch plays and soap operas that promote adultery, lust, and unfaithfulness.

Open your eyes and ears and take the time to hear His still small voice. Don't take lightly what the Lord shows you.

Challenge

Only we can choose what we see, hear, and even touch. Is there something that you are seeing, hearing, or doing that you like but you know that it is promoting wickedness?

Pray to the Lord right now and ask what is keeping you from walking closer to Him. Ask Him to show you if there is anything that you are watching, reading, doing, etc. that is not glorifying to Him and ask His forgiveness for it.

Try to also come up with alternative activities, books, or programs that will improve your spiritual walk.

LESSON 7

Don't Pick Them Back Up

"If my people, which are called by my name, shall humble themselves, and
pray, and seek my face, and turn from their wicked ways; then will I hear
from heaven, and will forgive their sin, and will heal their land."
(2 Chron. 7:14)

Sometimes we may ask, Why would the Lord choose me? I mess up so bad. At these times in our lives, we have to remember why Jesus came into the world. He did not come into the world for people who have it all together. He came to heal those who don't.

This next poem is for those who do their own laundry. Remember just as your laundry can be clean again, so are you by the Lord's precious blood.

Poem/Song

The Laundry Detergent Aisle
I got some verses that will make you smile.
come take a walk down the laundry detergent aisle.
When your sins like your laundry have piled up in stacks.
And waves of guilt come upon you in attacks.
And that guilt affects your life and you can't **Surf** the **Tide**.
And deep down from everyone you just want to hide.
Remember to stay Bold.
As you hear this story unfold.
Whether your sins were in this Era or back in the Seventh Generation.
His forgiveness is there whereever you Travelon to in this nation.
If you pour into your washer Ecover.
Open up His word and you will discover.
Whether you use Vaska, Nellies, Purex or Ivory Snow.
Remember that Jesus Christ is the great Dynamo.
Our God is Lord of the Sun & Earth.
And any other Planet you find of worth.
Whether you use Mrs. Meyer's, The Laundress, Prowash or Static Guard
Keep your eyes on Jesus when life starts to feel hard.

Whether you use Borax, Baby Ganics, or Scotch Guard.
He loves you whether you are washing shirts, pants or a leotard.
Whether you use Arm & Hammer, Dreft, Mio Fresh or Bi-O-Klean.
He cleans everywhere, even in between.
If you use Charlie's Soap, Mite Mix, Method or Oxyclean.
Jesus is Lord over things seen and unseen.
He will make you Martha Stewart Clean.
Jesus will wash your cares away better than Mr. Clean.
To live is Christ, to die is Gain.
He saved you by enduring that pain.
He took that sin from you to juggle.
So that when you get to Heaven you'll get a Snuggle.
In addition, He rose after His burial.
So rejoice like the little mermaid Ariel.
Jesus isn't just a religion or Fab.
Just Cheer, Shout, and be glad
While you measure that Niagra detergent by the ounce.
Remember Jesus gave you that Xtra Bounce.
When you drop in that Downy ball.
Remember that Jesus Christ paid for it All.
If you clean your clothes with Dropps.
Remember He saves all moms and pops.
Next time, you start worrying about your sin.
Remember through Jesus Christ we always Win.
Whether you wash your clothes day or night.
He will cleanse us from our sins like Woolite.
If you clean your clothes with Wisk.
Remember to Him it was well worth the risk.
Remember Our God is always Out of the Box.
His blood will bleach you white like Chlorox.

What Do You Think?

What makes sin so desirable? I hate to sin, so why do I fall away?

We try time and time again to turn from our sinful ways. It can be tough to talk about them sometimes. However, it is better to confess sin to Jesus in this life than to be punished for them in hell.

How does a man get to the point where he chooses to sin rather than listen to the Lord? Any sin is wrong. I pray to the Lord for deliverance from my sinful ways and for help overcoming temptations.

Why does sin appear so pleasing? Why do men remember that second of pleasure but forget the days of suffering that that sin has placed upon them?

It is hard not to sin when you have a lot going on in your life. The reason to commit any sin is always a lie. There is always that lie, "When I finish this, I will stop." Then five, ten, fifteen, twenty years pass and you are still committing that sin. Why do we rationalize sin?

The Lord rejoices when people confess their sins and leave their burdens at the cross. However, sometimes we pick our burdens back up and continue to sin against Him.

History repeats itself if we do not learn from our mistakes. If nothing is done about a person's sin, it will come back to haunt him at the worst possible time in his life.

This is why we must stop committing our sins, repent, and leave them at the cross!!!

The Lord wants to give us so much, and all we have to do is to give Him the unclean things in our lives. How can He make us brave if we still live in fear? How can we have wisdom if we still listen to foolishness? How can He give us joy if we do not have faith that He will deliver us? How can we expect to be helped if we do not help others?

I am a new creature in Christ. The old nature is no longer a part of my life. Resist the devil and he must flee. I will trust You, Lord. You are in control.

I need the Lord to help me resist my temptations. The Lord will deliver me through my trials and will give me the words to speak as He did for His disciples in the Bible.

Only through the Lord can I overcome my obstacles. I am a new creature. I must adopt different behaviors and patterns that will steer me clear of sin. As a new creature, I must present the image of Christ. I am a representative of God the Father and God the Son.

I have seen Him time and time again deliver me from evil despite my shortcomings. I must be a new creature for Him now so that I can be a new creature with a glorified body when I get to heaven.

This is why we must repent of our sins and turn to Him. We will only succeed through Him.

Challenge

Is there a sin that you can't seem to shake or that seems to win no matter how much you press into the Lord?

Thank the Lord for dying on cross for your sin. Confess it to the Lord and pray for deliverance from that sin.

While praying, it may be a good idea to break any generational curses that may have passed down from your family line all the way back to Adam and Eve. Also pray that the Lord will saturate your mind, body, soul, and spirit with His Holy Spirit and healing.

Remember that Jesus covered your sins when He died on the cross. You are a new creature in Christ.

I said, O my God, take me not away in the midst of my days:

thy years are throughout all generations.

Of old hast thou laid the foundation of the earth:

and the heavens are the work of thy hands.

They shall perish, but thou shalt endure: yea,

all of them shall wax old like a garment; as a vesture shalt thou change them, and they shall be changed:

But thou art the same, and thy years shall have no end.

The children of thy servants shall continue,

and their seed shall be established before thee.

(Psal. 102: 24-28)

LESSON 8

The Anchor

"A friend loveth at all times, and a brother is born for adversity," (Prov. 17:17)

Jesus is the best friend you will ever have. The Lord puts key people in your life to help share his love and friendship. We can learn a lot about the Lord and His love by looking at the family and friends that have an impact on our lives. True family and friends will be there for you in the good times and the bad.

I didn't have too many friends growing up. I thank the Lord for them. Friends are such a blessing, as one can see from this next Life Experience. Count yourself lucky if you had a lot of friends.

Life Exerience

Fortunately, the Lord gave me a very great friend. He and his family moved into the neighborhood. My cousin lived with my family at the time.

At the time, my day was just going to school, doing homework, and watching t.v. I was the biggest couch potato in the world.

My cousin was more outgoing than I was. I would hear him talk about my friend and his family when they first moved in. Through my cousin, I met one of my greatest friends.

We didn't start out as the best of friends right away. At first, I would only play with him when my cousin was around.

One day, my aunt came and took my cousin away. After he was gone, I went back to being a big couch potato. My friend would knock on the door every day. At first, I kept telling him I was busy watching t.v. Nevertheless, he still continued to knock on the door once a day.

Eventually, my conscience got the best of me. I went out with him once in a while to play with him just to shut him up. After a while, I started really having fun hanging out with him. Once in a while became every other day. Every other day turned into every day. Eventually we became great friends.

One thing I really admired about my friend's family was the way his parents always spent time with him. My dad, when he was off, used to just watch TV and not spend a lot of time with the rest of the family. My friend's dad played sports and other games with us. He even took me with them on trips when they went to Lake George, New York, and other places. My friend's house was like my second home.

I also admired how, with so many making fun of me, he still stuck with me. I'm sure lots of people came up to him and asked him why he hung out with me.

My friend also helped me to realize that there was more to life than watching t.v. Life is too short in this world. I realized that there was so much to do outside. My friend helped me to stay active.

I thank the Lord for a great friend who didn't give up on me. Because he didn't give up on me, I can't give up on him. He is so important to me. I hope that I can be together with all of my friends and family someday in Heaven.

What Do You Think?

The Lord made every creature. He turns the old into new. He is Lord through the busy times. He is Lord through the times of peace.

Think of all the changes that have happened. We are no longer riding horses to get around. Almost every home in America has a t.v. We have computers that can fit into the palms of our hands.

So many advances in technology, yet the hearts of people have fallen away. I believe that no matter how advanced technology gets, we will never be able to control the weather, define true love, or wipe away every tear.

The Lord brings joy and peace to those who seek Him. The devil is always looking to bring us back into sin. We need to keep the Lord ahead of us and stay focused on him.

He is the anchor in my life. Even when gravity ceases to exist, it rains fire from the sky, or pancakes grow on trees, the Lord is still the same yesterday, today, and forever.

Challenge

> "I will love thee, O Lord, my strength. The Lord is my rock, and my fortress, and my deliverer; my God, my strength, in whom I will trust; my buckler, and the horn of my salvation, and my high tower." (Psal. 18: 1-2)

We need the love of Jesus. Without the Lord, how is a man to survive or stand? We will go the way of dinosaurs if the Lord is not in our lives.

Think of a situation that you or a friend is currently worried about and ask the Lord to remove any fear and worry associated with that situation. Thank the Lord that He is your strength and your Deliverer. Pray believing that the Lord is all powerful. Trust the Lord even when things look bad.

LESSON 9

The Fourth Grade Assignment

"These things I have spoken unto you, that in me ye might have peace. In the world ye shall have tribulation: but be of good cheer; I have overcome the world." (John 16: 33)

We are called to share the Bible with everyone. However, sometimes when we step out in faith and share the Gospel, there is always going to be opposition. There will always be people who will think you are nuts or they will criticize your walk with the Lord.

In this poem, there are two speakers. Speaker 1 is someone who is sharing about the Lord. Speaker 2 is an antagonist who hates the Word of God and will try his best to stop the Word from being proclaimed.

Poem/Song

Keep Quiet

Speaker 1:

Why is it when you want to talk about the Lord.
The one who should be most adored.
There is always that one person around.
That tries to plant your feet back on the ground.

Speaker 2:

Not so Loud!!

Speaker 1:

Why is it when you preach about Jesus to a crowd.

Speaker 2:

SSSSSHHHHHHHHHHHHHHHHHHHHHHHHHHHHH

Speaker 1:

How he died, was risen, and ascended up into a cloud.

Speaker 2:

SSSSSHHHHHHHHHHHHHHHHHHHHHHHH

Speaker 1:

That you hear that hushing sound.

Speaker 2:

Keep it Down!!!

Speaker 1:

Let the world know that Jesus saves.
He can raise people from the graves.
He can heal cancer, pneumonia, and aids.
He can heal our souls, hearts, and pains.

Speaker 2:

Leave your faith at home preacher!!

Speaker 1:

There is a lesson that I have to teach ya.
Not everyone is going to like what you have to say.
Remember the world hated Him first so don't be gray.
We are called to be a light to this world.
The Lord wants us to witness to every boy and girl.

Speaker 2:

Separation of Church and State!!!

Speaker 1:

Now that is a statement that makes me irate.
Especially since it is so abused,
Because the world is so confused.
This simply says we do not discriminate,
And use religion in order to hate.

Speaker 2:

Zip It!!

Speaker 1:

We need to open up our mouths and rip it,

And not lose our freedom under the first amendment,
Which helps us speak boldly like a flight attendant.

Speaker 2:

Shut Up!!

Speaker 1:

So when you're ready to give up,
Remember, the enemy is like a flood.
Our fight is not with flesh and blood.
But with the principalities of the air.
The Devil is like a lion or a bear.
In the name of Jesus you have to go.

Speaker 2:

Oh Nooooooooooooooooooooooooooo!!

Speaker 1:

I don't mean to cause a riot.
But remember when you are told to be quiet.
Look to Jesus when the world gets violent.
Speak boldly and don't be silent.

Life Experience:

I continued to excel in my schoolwork through second, third, and fourth grade. It was not always easy.

I remember one time in fourth grade when I had to do an assignment. I had to write down what I would wish for if I had three wishes. One of my wishes was to see Jesus so that I could thank Him for everything He has done for me.

When the teacher looked at it, she crumbled up the paper and screamed "What's wrong with you. Do you mean that you want to die?" They called the psychologist into the class and we all sat down and had a big group discussion.

It is not easy being a kid with everyone staring at you thinking that you're nuts. However, I got a chance to tell them about Jesus. It is not easy at the time being used by the Lord, but afterwards, you can look back and see what the Lord was trying to do in your life.

Challenge

If you were brought to court because you were accused of being a Christian, would there be enough evidence to convict you?

The Lord is looking for people who will step out and proclaim His name to the nations. Ask the Lord to give you the boldness and wisdom to proclaim His name as He did for the disciples. Pray that the Lord will give you divine appointments to speak to others about Jesus and His wonderful love.

LESSON 10
My Friend from Fifth Grade

"Honor thy father and thy mother: that thy days may be long upon the land which the Lord thy God giveth thee." (Exod. 20:12)

The Lord has the best intentions for us. Even with our sin, the Lord still wanted us to be with Him. That is why He sent His son to die on the cross.

This next poem is about the perfect gift that Jesus gave. He is the best friend any of us could ever have.

Poem/Song

Perfect Gifts
In life, the best gifts
are the ones that give you lifts.
The perfect gift of all was Christ's love
That flows down from Heaven like a dove.
He died on the cross that I may live.
What more than a life can one give?
He was bound so that I could be free.
He gave us light so we could see.
He was wounded so that I could heal.
He was imprisoned to give us an appeal.
He was mocked so that we could give praise.
He was torn down to give us a raise.
He suffered the pain of being rejected
So that by God we could be accepted.
He wore that crown of thorns.
To get us through life's storms.
In three days He rose from the dead
So death is no longer a thing to dread.
Everlasting life with Him.
And deliverance from our sin.
The second perfect gift is a friend

Who will be there for us till the end.
Someone who will meet you halfway
And be there to celebrate your birthday.
I thank the Lord and everyone for being here.
To me, all of you are so very dear.

Life Experience

For fifth grade, my mom wanted my sister and me to go to Upton Lake Christian Academy. This was a private Christian school near Salt Point, New York.

It was here that I met another great friend of mine. He had an older sister and a younger sister. The older sister became great friends with my sister.

This friend was a very nice guy. It was great to have another friend I could talk to about the Lord and what He was doing in my life.

His father and mother were great parents. His father was a pastor at a Methodist church. I liked his church services.

Unfortunately, they lived about an hour away. I could only hang out with him at school and every couple of weekends, when either I would go over to his house or he would come over to ours.

I enjoyed going to this school. I was no longer in special needs classes. I was in a class that had a normal program for a fifth grader. I continued to do well and I was on the honor roll.

This was a very rough time for my mom, since she worked twelve- hour shifts at a power plant. The school was an hour away, so we could not get a bus to pick us up. My mom worked, drove to and from the school, and still took the time to take us on hiking trips, clean the house, and do the shopping. She did all this on four hours of sleep each day or less.

We do not realize all that our parents do for us. This is why it is so important to honor your parents.

Challenge

Parents are not perfect, and they do make bad decisions. However, you will never find people on the planet who love you as much as they do.

Like God, true parents have plans to help you and not to harm you. We must honor our parents as we must honor God, who is Father to us all. Take this time to thank your parents for giving birth to you and for raising you. Ask the Lord to help you forgive your parents for any poor decisions and actions.

Take this time to also thank the Lord for dying on the cross for your sins.
Take a few minutes to listen for His still small voice.

Be not thou afraid when one is made rich,

when the glory of his house is increased;

For when he dieth he shall carry nothing away:

his glory shall not descend after him.

Though while he lived he blessed his soul:

and men will praise thee, when thou doest well to thyself.

He shall go to the generation of his fathers;

they shall never see light.

Man that is in honour, and understandeth not,

is like the beasts that perish.

(Psal. 49: 16-20)

LESSON 11

Pray for the Rich and Famous

"Then said Jesus unto his disciples, Verily I say unto you, That a rich man shall hardly enter into the kingdom of heaven. And again I say unto you, It is easier for a camel to go through the eye of a needle, than for a rich man to enter into the kingdom of God." (Matt. 19: 23-24)

Gossip is a very deadly sin that is crippling the churches. Like lust, it is a silent killer. People don't see the harm in it because they see it as nothing more than a little white lie. As I mentioned previously, all sin is wrong whether it is lying or murder.

Gossip really cripples growth in the body of Christ. How can people feel free to worship the Lord when people are gossiping about them and judging them.

In this next poem, there are three speakers. The first speaker is the main character. Speakers two and three are two gossips gossiping about Speaker 1 while he is speaking.

Poem/Song

Buzybody Bees

Speaker 1:

Beware of busybody bees
They can be as harmful as fleas.
They don't produce any honey.
But what they say about you may not be funny.

Speaker 2:

Bz Bz Bz

Speaker 3:

Bz Bz Bz

Speaker 1:

They criticize your Holy Spirit walk.
They slander the Body of Christ as they talk.
I don't want to see anyone stung.
So focus on the Lord and watch your tongue.

Speaker 2:

Bz Bz Bz

Speaker 3:

Bz Bz Bz

Speaker 1:

Those busybody bees may not fly.
But those busybody bees are very sly.
They will make fun of people old and new.
They will make up rumors that aren't true.

Speaker 2:

Bz Bz Bz

Speaker 3:

Bz Bz Bz

Speaker 1:

Instead of receiving people in Christ's love.
Any body not in their clique, they give the shove.
Those busybody bees may not have stingers.
But with their tongues they provoke with zingers.

Speaker 2:

Bz Bz Bz

Speaker 3:

Bz Bz Bz

Speaker 1:

Gossiping is a deadly sin.
It keeps people from knowing Him.
How can they know that Christ cares,
When people are judging them with their stares?

Speaker 2:

Bz Bz Bz

Speaker 3:

Bz Bz Bz

Speaker 1:

Don't be part of the busybody beehive.
The love of Christ, gossip will deprive.
Don't be quick to hear the buzz.
Don't worry about what he or she does.

Speaker 2:

Bz Bz Bz

Speaker 3:

Bz Bz Bz

Speaker 1:

We are called to be a light.
Don't speak against people, it isn't right.
Just think about what the Lord has for you.
Don't partake in gossip, stick to what is true.

Speaker 2:

Bz Bz Bz

Speaker 3:

Bz Bz Bz

What Do You Think?

Everyone needs prayer sometimes. Prayer helps us to stay focused on the Lord. It is how the Lord speaks to His people.

Our entertainers, celebrities, and people in high places need prayer just as much as a homeless person on the street. They may have riches and fame but they don't know about Jesus. Because of this, they have nothing.

Forgive me for coveting their riches and for letting that keep me from praying for them. Should I let their riches keep me from forgiving them when I hear of what they do on the news? Forgive me for not stopping the gossip about celebrities and for not praying for them when they go through trials.

We need to keep our bosses, Presidents, and leaders in prayer and forgive them for their bad decisions. Pray that the truth will be known to them and that they will take a stand for what is right. In order for our leaders and celebrities to take a stand for what is right, we need to take the first step because we know Jesus but a lot of them don't.

Without Jesus, people have no idea of what is right and what is wrong. Pray. Don't gossip when you hear of people in trouble. Let not their success keep envy in your heart.

Do not covet and keep envy toward people who have what you don't have. You have the one thing everyone needs. That is Jesus Christ in your heart.

Challenge

Do you let what material possessions and talents people have keep you from befriending them and praying for them? When you hear of people in trouble, instead of praying for them, do you go and blab about their situation to other people and judge them?

Ask the Lord to show you people you are envious of, and ask Him to remove envy from you.

Think about all the celebrities and people that you hear about on the news who are going through trials. Please take some time to pray for them.

LESSON 12
The Kid with the Bubble Gum

"If any man serve me, let him follow me; and where I am, there shall also
my servant be: if any man serve me, him will my Father honour."
(John 12:26)

If God was real, why doesn't He just appear and prove to everyone that He is God? Why does God allow all the debate that goes on in the world concerning His existence?

Why do you believe in God? People believe that God exists for different reasons. Some reasons can sound more unusual then others as one will see in this next life experience.

Life Experience

One day, I was waiting at a train station with a friend of mine. My friend asked me why I believe that God exists. I told him that I believe in God because the Lord helps me get through each and every day. He healed my brain when everyone else told me I was retarded.

My friend then said he believes in God because if he were God, he wouldn't let people know He exists.

At first, this sounded weird to me. My friend then gave an example of a kid in class who had bubble gum. If the kid told the whole class that he had bubble gum, then everyone would demand that he share a piece with them, whether they wanted to be friends with him or not.

However, if the kid with the gum keeps quiet about it, he can have plenty of gum for his true friends and himself. He would know his true friends, because they would like him for who he is and not just because he has gum.

My friend said that was why he believes God is real. Jesus is that kid in class with the gum. He wants to see if we accept Him for who He is and not just because we can get stuff from Him. He wants people who choose to follow Him simply because He is God.

What Do You Think?

Sometimes we think God should be a genie who just appears on call and grants our every wish. If Jesus did everything we asked, would we really worship Him as God or would we just continue to try to boss Him around like a slave?

Jesus wants friends, not bullies who just demand gum and lunch money from Him. Sometimes we think we can bully God. Sometimes we try to bully Him by cheating with our tithes, or "threaten" Him with not going to church or helping anyone in need until we get what we want from Him. Some people even put Him in a dress and call Him "**she**" or "**it**" instead of "**He**," just to fit their own little preferences of who they think God should be.

There is one flaw with this way of thinking in the life experience. It assumes that God does not want us to know He exists. The good news is that God does want to show us how real He is, not by being a doormat who gives us whatever we want, but by revealing Himself to us through the Bible, through time in prayer, through worship, and through others who also know Him.

He also reveals Himself to us in our trials. These are the times in our lives when no one else will stand by us. These are the times when everyone else is ashamed to be with us. Thank God that He is there with us.

It is just amazing that God would leave the joy, peace, love, magnificence, and safety of Heaven, where everyone praises Him around the clock, to come to earth, where people reject Him, mock Him, and disobey His commandments, just to spend time with me.

Challenge

As mentioned earlier, people believe in God for many different reasons. However, in the end they all lead to the same conclusion. That God is real.

Ask yourself why you believe God exists. Think of all the times that the Lord has revealed Himself to You. Ask the Lord for wisdom on what to say when people ask you this question.

Was there ever a time in your life when you tried to tell God what to do? Ask the Lord to forgive you for being a bully and honor Him as your God and friend.

LESSON 13

Christmas is for Everyone

"Glory to God in the highest, and on earth peace, good will toward men."
(Luke 2: 14)

The main reason for Christmas should be to celebrate Christ coming into the world. Sometimes we get so caught up in the presents, the parties, and Santa Clause, that we miss the most important meaning of the holiday season.

It is almost a crime to say "Merry Christmas" to someone. People for centuries have been trying to change Christmas into something else, like Xmas or Happy Holidays.

During Christmas, you see a million people dressed up as Santa Clause. How many people dress up as Jesus. Where are the lines to see Jesus during the Christmas season?

In this next poem, there are four speakers; the Announcer, Santa Clause,

Jesus Christ, and the Narrator. I hope this poem allows you to see the true meaning of Christmas.

Poem/Song

Christmas Debate

Announcer:

Welcome to the National Christmas Debate,
To determine whose name is on the December 25th date.
In the ring, we have two contenders.
They will debate their case as defenders.
For the one corner, put together your hands and paws.
It is jolly old Saint Nick, Santa Clause
(Clapping)
In the other corner, let's hear a Noel.
It is Jesus Christ, the Prince of Peace, Emmanuel.
(Clapping)

41

Narrator:

Santa without hesitation stepped first up on the stage.
Shaking like a bowl full of jelly, Santa prepared to engage.

Santa Clause:

Ho Ho Ho.
You better not pout, you better not cry.
You better not pout, cause I'm tellin you why.
To change Christmas to Clausmas is what I vote.
I will tell you why in just one note.
I heard this Nazarene say that all of you are evil and no good.
Vote for Him and all you get is coal instead of presents like you should.
Vote for me and I will give you a treat.
Candy, toys, presents, and things that are neat.
I will give you so much more if I could.
Because I say that all of you are so good!
I am Santa Clause and I approve this message.
(Clapping)

Narrator:

Santa walked off the stage and sat in a chair.
To the crowd, what Santa said seemed fair.
Jesus Christ got up and walked onto the stand.
Full of love, He spoke as He waved His hand.

Jesus Christ:

I'll tell you why I should be the reason
Why I am the reason for this holiday season.
Because you inherited Adam and Eve's sinful gene.
I stepped out of Heaven onto that manger scene.
I knew I would be beaten and rejected in this world.
But I did it anyway so that I could save every boy and girl.
So that God, My Father, can see you like He should.
He will see Me in you and He will say "that's good!!"
I give you more than just material things.
So let us hear all those jingle bell's rings.
I bring Joy, Peace, Goodness, and Love.
These are precious gifts straight from Heaven above.
So along with the tree when you put out that Manger.
Remember how I serve and protect you as a ranger.
I will defeat the Devil and save you out of any danger.

Just invite me in, I won't force myself like a stranger.
In the name of God the Father, God the Son, and the Holy Ghost,
We approve this message.
(Clapping and Cheering)

Announcer:

I think it is crystal clear.
Let Christ's name be on this day of cheer.
Merry Christmas to each and every one.
Because the # One we are celebrating is God's Son.
(Clapping and Cheering)

What Do You Think?

Christmas is the day we celebrate when the Lord came into the world in the form of a baby. To some of us, this is a joyous occasion. To other people, this is a day no different from any other day.

Some people wake up and there are no presents under the tree. There is no turkey or ham to eat. There are no loved ones stopping by to see them. They have nobody around and no place to go to for Christmas.

To some people, Christmas can be a very depressing time of the year. Some people have lost loved ones. Because of this, their Christmas is never the same.

Take joy on this day. Not because of presents, but because through Jesus we are free from our sins. Thank the Lord for our families, friends, and land.

It is easy to wish "Merry Christmas" to people who love you. However, you should also wish "Merry Christmas" to your enemies and people you don't really know. You should give a gift to someone who cannot give you something in return.

When Jesus died on the cross, He gave us the perfect gift. There is no way we can repay the Lord for what He has done. Jesus knows that, but He still loves us and is generous to us.

There are some people who spend Christmas alone simply because they have not forgiven their family members or friends. Don't let unforgiveness rob you of your Christmas joy. In fact, don't wait until Christmas to forgive your brother or sister. Don't let the sun go down with hate for people in your heart. The world has suffered enough from unforgiveness through spoken and unspoken words, crimes, murders, wars, and tragedies.

Christmas is for everyone, not just for you. Come let us adore Him together.

Challenge

Take some time to read the first two chapters of Matthew and Luke. As you read the accounts of the birth of Jesus, ask yourself what similarities and differences there are between the two accounts. What was the author trying to portray about Jesus in each account?

Also try one Christmas, to give a gift to an enemy, a person you don't know, a poor person, an elderly person, a ministry, and a neighbor. Try and do this at least one Christmas in your lifetime.

The gift does not have to be something material. It can be your time, your friendship, or even just saying the words, "I forgive you" or "Jesus loves you." These two statements can turn the whole world upside down. Jesus is looking for people willing to do this.

Finally, brethren, pray for us,

that the Word of the Lord may have free course, and be glorified, even as it is with you:

And that we may be delivered from unreasonable and wicked men:

from all men have not faith.

But the Lord is faithful,

who shall establish you, and keep you from evil.

And we have confidence in the Lord touching you,

that ye both do and will do the things which we command you.

And the Lord direct your hearts into the love of God,

and into the patient waiting for Christ.

(2 Thes. 3: 1-5)

LESSON 14
Different Churches

"We then, as workers together with Him, beseech you also that ye receive
not the grace of God in vain." (2 Cori. 6:1)

Do you know that the Lord hates religion? It keeps people from really knowing who He is. The Lord is more than manmade traditions and rules. Being religious and having a personal relationship with the Lord are two different things.

Religion uses works and man-made laws to try and worship the Lord. Having a personal relationship with Jesus is to not only obey Him but to love him and his creation with all of your heart, soul, and spirit. Religion works to divide. Jesus looks to unite the body.

The Pharisees in the days of Jesus' life on earth had religion, but their hearts were far from knowing Him. The biggest opposition to His ministry came from religious leaders. This next poem shows how destructive religion can be. Along with the chorus, there is a dance much like the Electric Slide.

Poem/Song

The Pharisee Slide
Welcome to the council of the Pharisees and Scribes.
We stand for religion to all Israel's twelve tribes.
We rely on our works and the praises of men.
In public we pronounce hallelujah and amen.
But if you want to be a real Pharisee or Scribe.
You have to know how to do the Pharisee slide.

Chorus

**You have to
walk this way (slide to the left)
Talk this way (slide to the right)
Think this way(left hand points to head)
Act this way(right hand points to head)**

Put that money in the collection plate.
Flap like a dove. (flap arms like a bird)
Fit as a glove. (hug yourself)
Act this way (cross arms)
Make sure you pay.
And do whatever
we say. (face left and bob up and down)
Dum Dum Dum Dum Dum Dum
Dum Dum Dum Dum Dum Dum
What we say (face right and bob up and down)
Dum Dum Dum Dum Dum Dum
Dum Dum Dum Dum Dum Dum
One day, a man named Jesus appeared.
This man we really hated and feared
Because the people turned to Him
And He dares to tell us that we sin.
How we rob and steal using God's house.
We agreed to exterminate Him like a mouse.
This guy gives our religion a bad vibe.
And tells people not to do our Pharisee slide.

Chorus

Jesus on the Sabbath heals.
And He rebukes all our religious appeals.
He exposes all our scams and lies.
So we plot the way He dies.
Jesus is more than religion and rules.
He is making us look like fools.
So together we scheme and jibe.
to the beat of the Pharisee slide.

Chorus

As Jesus continues to show His love,
To our religion, people give it the shove.
Our works don't get us to Heaven, He will say.
But He claims He is the only way.
We find no fault in this Rabbi.
So we need to be really sly.
But no matter how hard with our questions we try,
He always leaves us speechless with His replies.
We must overcome Him like a tide.
So that we can save our Pharisee slide.

Chorus

One day His disciple named Judas Iscariot
Came to us with news like a golden chariot.
He gave us all much bliss.
That He would betray Jesus with a kiss.
We picked up Jesus in a garden
And from death we would not pardon.
We beat Him, kick Him, and abuse,
Even though our accusations are untrue.
To the dance floor we must glide.
He is dead, now do the Pharisee slide.

Chorus

After three days came the guards we paid.
They said the ground shook where His body laid.
The stone was rolled away.
And Jesus came out better than okay.
Uh Oh we all thought.
So to this lie we all sought.
We instructed the guards to say
That at night, the disciples took the body away.
So to save our religion we killed and we lied.
All we have to comfort us is our Pharisee Slide.

Chorus

Today, people and churches still do the Pharisee slide.
And use religion so that from the Lord they hide.
Man's law instead of God's law they choose.
And God's wisdom they mock and abuse.
They are so busy fitting in like a glove
We forget the most important is to share God's love.
For His love and guidance we must strive,
And forget the religious Pharisee Slide
Dum Dum Dum Dum Dum Dum
Dum Dum Dum Dum Dum Dum
Dum Dum Dum Dum Dum Dum
Dum Dum Dum Dum Dum Dum.

Life Experience

My family went to a lot of different churches when I was growing up. Each one had a different way of serving the Lord.

After my mom got saved, my mom, my sister, and I went to a Baptist church in Newburgh, New York. This was a very nice church. During this time, my mom continued to press into the Bible and continued to grow.

My mom noticed that the people in the church kept saying the gifts of the Spirit were not for today. This grieved her, because the gifts of the Spirit are meant especially for today and especially for us.

Anyway, we decided to find a different church. I remembered a church that she took us to for vacation Bible school in Hopewell Junction, New York. My mom, my sister, and I decided to give it a try. At this church, people danced and sang to the worship music. They believed in the gifts of the Spirit. My dad did not go to church with us since he went to a Catholic church near where we lived.

My mom wanted dad to feel the same joy that we experienced at our church. She prayed about it and the Lord gave her a great idea. We would go with my dad to his church and then he would come with us to ours. My dad agreed, and we went as a family to the two churches.

Eventually, dad told mom that we did not have to come with him to his church anymore, but he would still go with us. He stopped going to his church. He said that he just didn't feel love at his church like he did at ours.

I am not saying that going to a Catholic church is bad. I am saying that you have to go where you feel the love of Jesus, the presence of the Holy Spirit, and the desire to keep the Lord's commandments and words close to your heart.

I got baptized and I also received the Holy Spirit into my life. My whole family continued to grow spiritually together.

Challenge

When I talk about the gifts of the Spirit, I am talking about the gifts of healing, prophecy, tongues, preaching, and teaching.

Jesus healed people when He was on the earth. The disciples, by the power of the Holy Spirit, healed people even after Jesus was taken up into heaven. Jesus is the same today as He was back then.

Sometimes we limit God and we don't realize all the power He has. We need to remind ourselves that He is a mighty God. He can heal anyone.

Ask the Lord for a personal relationship with Him. When you ask, pray to be baptized in the Holy Spirit and ask Him to show you what your gifts are. God desires that all of his people have the power and authority to heal the sick and to stand against the Devil's devices. The gifts of the Spirit are especially for today.

LESSON 15
His Faithfulness

"God is faithful, by whom ye were called unto the fellowship of his Son
Jesus Christ our Lord." (I Cori. 1:9)

Our God is amazing. Our God can do great things. Sometimes we doubt His power. We have to keep declaring the promises of the Lord over our situations and continue to trust Him. Faith is the belief in things that are unseen. We need to keep our faith in the Lord.

This next poem is about the story of Joshua and his battle against Jericho. It took Joshua a lot of faith to believe that the Lord would bring those walls down. As you read this, think about a situation you may be going through which seems hopeless. Remember, the Lord will never leave you nor forsake you.

Poem/Song

WOW
Here is a story that most of you know,
How the Lord helped Joshua take Jericho.
Jericho was a city surrounded by a wall.
And armed men patrolled every hall.
Now the Lord told Joshua that he gave them the town.
He said "Those walls will fall to the ground."
The Lord said for six days go once around,
Then on the seventh, seven times go around.
After this, tell the people to give a shout,
And you will see my glory and take those people out.
Joshua believed. He cast out all fear and doubt.
He thought of this song believing these things would come about.

Chorus

Wow wow wee, Wow wow wow!!
God has broken those walls down.
God has given us the town.

Wow wow wee, Wow wow wow!!
Give a cheer, Give a shout.
Give Him all your fear and doubt.
Wow wow wee, Wow wow wow!!
God is good, God is great.
It is time to celebrate.
Wow wow wee Wow wow wow!!
Oh His Glory will astound.
Wow Wow Wee Wow Wow Wow!!
Wow Wow Wee Wow Wow Wow!!
Joshua and the people started right away.
They marched around that wall that first day.
As they marched, they wondered why.
While they looked to the Lord in the sky.
Not a word was said.
They went full speed ahead.
Joshua continued to cast out all fear and doubt.
He thought of this song to sing when these things come about.

Chorus

On the second and third day
The men of Jericho started to play.
They teased and taunted as Israel marched.
Marching was tough, the men were parched.
"What are you doing", the men of Jericho bellowed and cried.
The Israelites just wanted to turn around and hide.
The people started to question within.
If they truly heard from Him.
Those walls were looking mighty big.
As those men continued to taunt and jig.
Joshua looked to the Lord to cast out all fear and doubt.
He thought of the song to sing when these things come about.

Chorus

Day four, five, and six the same thing.
Each day the people did not talk or sing.
Tomorrow, they would march around seven times.
Then the people could sing those powerful rhymes.
Joshua started to shake slightly in fear.
Oh how he wished Moses was here.

Then he remembered how for them the Jordan cleared.
Just like the Red Sea for Moses, it adhered.
Joshua looked to the Lord to cast out all fear and doubt.
He thought of the song to sing knowing it would come about.

Chorus

Day seven was finally here,
Time to cast out all doubt and fear.
Around and around the Israelites went,
wondering if those walls even had a dent.
Nevertheless, the marching they continued to do.
Believing that God's word was true.
After the seventh time, the horns were blown.
The people shouted and this was known,
Those walls just came tumbling down.
The men of Jericho began to frown.
Joshua conquered the city and took it out.
He sang this song with a cheer and a shout.

Chorus

Remember when the Lord gives you something to do,
Remember to trust in the Lord who is always true,
Don't listen when you hear words of fear and doubt.
Ask the Lord to cast those thoughts out.
When you doubt and ask "How?"
The Lord will leave you saying "WOW"
Wow Wow Wee Wow Wow Wow!!
Wow Wow Wee Wow Wow Wow!!

Life Experience

The Lord was so faithful in my life when I was a child. Here are a few of the many examples of His faithfulness.

There was a huge pine tree that my cousin, my friends, and I would use as a tree fort. This tree was bigger than a house.

One day, my cousin and I climbed up to the very top of the tree. When we started down the tree, I slipped off a branch and I fell. I did not hit any branches until I got to the very bottom of the tree. I hit one branch before I hit the ground. That branch broke my fall.

I heard my cousin screaming. I tried to speak but nothing would come out. I was terrified. After a minute of trying to say something, I slowly got my voice back.

I was able to get up and tell my parents what had happened. I did not have to go to the hospital. I did not have one thing wrong with me from the fall.

Here is another example of the Lord's faithfulness. On my eighth birthday. I had my party at a roller rink.

I was sitting on a bench waiting to go home. I saw my dad sitting across from me. I started to daydream. When I snapped out of it, I saw that my dad was gone.

I looked around for him. I went outside and looked down the hill. I saw my dad drive away with some of my friends.

My parents had taken two cars to the party since they had picked up my friends and driven them to the roller rink. Each of my parents thought I was with the other.

I stared down the hill in disbelief. I knew how to get home, so I started walking. I should have stayed, but I was in shock from being left behind.

I managed to cross two lanes of traffic. People stopped and asked me if I needed a ride. My mom had warned me about going with strangers, so I didn't go with them. One man pulled up in a van and tried to grab me. I ran by him and kept running and didn't look back. I believe that man was trying to kidnap me, but the Lord protected me.

I almost got to a 7-11 before I saw a red Chevy Nova pull over. My dad got out. I was so happy to see him! I ran up to my dad and hugged him.

We went back to the roller rink, because my mom was frantically searching for me there. We picked her up and went home, where my sister, grandma, and cousin were waiting for us.

Here is the final example of the Lord's faithfulness I am going to share. One night, one of my friends came over for the weekend and we had a sleepover. We used to have an old mattress downstairs. When my parents went to bed, we put it on the stairs and slid down it like a slide.

I grabbed a pillow. I was going to jump onto the pillow and land on the mattress. Instead, I jumped clear over the pillow, over the mattress, and into the wall downstairs.

My left arm really hurt. I did not tell my mom until a day later.

Sunday morning, I was in tears. We were on our way to church. My parents, seeing the expression on my face, asked me what was wrong. I couldn't take the pain anymore, so I told them.

Instead of going to church, we went to the hospital. The doctor took some x-rays of my arm. After looking at them, he said that I was going to need surgery. He also said that I would lose some stretch in my arm.

When the doctor left the room, my mom and I prayed. I did not want to have surgery and I was desperately asking the Lord for help.

When he came back, the doctor decided to take more x-rays. After the second set, he looked at those x-rays. He then looked back at the first set. Then he looked at the second, and back at the first set again.

He must have looked back and forth at those x-rays for about ten or fifteen minutes while scratching his head. He said "I don't understand. I see a major break in the first set but I don't see it in the second set."

I still had to wear a cast but I was glad that I didn't have to have surgery. My arm healed properly and I have full use of it to this very day.

Challenge

Read Joshua Chapter 6. As you read this, think about times in your life that the Lord delivered you from a situation that seemed hopeless.

> *Pray to the Lord to help remove fear and doubt. Remember, if we have the faith of a mustard seed, we can say to that mountain "Move and be cast into the sea!" and it will obey. All things are possible with God.*

For I through the law am dead to the law,

that I might live unto God.

I am crucified with Christ: nevertheless I live;

yet not I, but Christ liveth in me: and the life which I now live in the flesh I live by the faith of the Son of God, who loved me, and gave himself for me.

I do not frustrate the grace of God:

for if righteousness come by the law, then Christ is dead in vain.

(Gala. 2: 19-21)

LESSON 16
The Legal Clause

"And by Him all that believe are justified from all things, from which ye
could not be justified by the law of Moses." (Acts 13: 39)

No matter how good we try to be, we are still condemned by our sins. Even if we commit one
sin, no matter how good we are, we will never pay off the debt caused by that one sin, no matter
how small it may be in our eyes. We all fall short of the glory of God.

This next poem is about the story of Moses and the ten commandments. When the
Lord first gave Moses the ten commandments, there was no grace or mercy for our sins. We
are condemned by the law. Fortunately, the Lord sent His son into the world to suffer the
punishment that we all deserve under the law.

Poem/Song

Countdown
In the book of Exodus Chapter Twenty
On the way to the land flowing with milk and honey,
The Lord gave Moses and Israel's clans
Etched in stone ten commands.
Moses read commandment number one,
To worship no other but God the Father, Spirit, and Son.
This command was declared all around.
The people of God joined in the countdown.
One,
one

Chorus

**It all comes down to one.
The Father, Spirit, Son
Give the Lord all your heart.
Your soul and mind and every part.
One, one**

It all comes down to one.
The Father, Spirit, Son.
The Father Spirit Son.
Moses read commandment number two,
Worshipping people and things you just don't do.
Don't worship trees or animals in the zoo.
Don't worship earthly knowledge like Timbuktu.
This command was declared all around.
The people of God joined in the countdown.
two, one,
one

Chorus

Moses read commandment number three,
Don't use the Lord's name for profanity.
Watch your mouth when talking about thee.
Use His name to bless, not for adversity.
This command was declared all around.
The people of God joined in the countdown.
three, two, one,
one ·

Chorus

Moses read commandment number four,
Remember on the Sabbath to adore.
Remember on the Sabbath to do no chore.
Rest and think of the Lord at the day's core.
This command was declared all around.
The people of God joined in the countdown.
four, three, two, one,
one

Chorus

Moses read commandment number five,
The honor of your pop and mom don't deprive.
Follow this and the longer you're alive.
Keep this, so your parents don't take a dive.
This command was declared all around.
The people of God joined in the countdown.

five, four, three, two, one,
one

Chorus

Moses read commandment number six,
Not to kill anyone just for kicks.
This is one that sticks.
It keeps us from becoming lunatics.
This command was declared all around.
The people of God joined in the countdown.
six, five, four, three, two, one,
one

Chorus

Moses read commandment number seven,
Don't commit adultery, which keeps you from Heaven.
Unless married, don't open yourself up like a 7-11.
Don't defile your body, be like bread that's unleavened.
This command was declared all around.
The people of God joined in the countdown.
seven, six, five, four, three, two, one,
one

Chorus

Moses read commandment number eight,
Stealing things makes God irate.
Don't take another person or company's freight.
Robbing God and others you are to hate.
This command was declared all around.
The people of God joined in the countdown.
eight, seven, six, five, four, three, two, one,
one

Chorus

Moses read commandment number nine,
Do not bear false witness which could confine.
Speaking falsely against your neighbor is not fine.
This grieves the Lord down to the spine.
This command was declared all around.
The people of God joined in the countdown.
nine, eight, seven, six, five, four, three, two, one,
one

Chorus

Moses read commandment number ten,
Do not covet any women or men.
Do not covet your neighbor's house or den.
His money, his goods, not now, not then.
This command was declared all around.
The people of God joined in the countdown.
ten, nine, eight, seven, six, five, four, three, two, one,

one

Chorus

If you think this is the end, think again.
Remember Jesus Christ, our biggest fan.
He died on the cross to free us of sin.
The law's curse is broken so we can be with Him.
However, this does not mean that it's okay.
To break these commandments and disobey.
Jesus came to fulfill and not to repeal.
His commandments we need to embrace and seal.
This command was declared all around.
The people of God joined in the countdown.
ten, nine, eight, seven, six, five, four, three, two, one,

one

Chorus

It all comes down to One.

Life Experience

After driving us for a year to and from Upton Lake Christian Academy, my mom realized she was too stressed out to keep driving an hour there and an hour back. She decided to put my sister and me into a Christian private school that was closer to us and provided a bus to pick us up and drop us back home.

There was a private Christian school in Poughkeepsie, New York. I went there from sixth to eighth grade. I am not going to disclose the name of the school.

This school was very legalistic and lacked the mercy of Jesus. Students received detentions for not wearing a belt or forgetting to wear a tie to chapel. I received a couple of detentions for forgetting my tie or my belt.

It was an environment where people would look for any imperfection in you and would talk about you behind your back. Even the teachers were like that. One time, I brought in a tube of Pringles potato chips for lunch. The teacher offered to give me a dollar for it. I had plenty of food for lunch and very little money, since I never got paid an allowance, so I agreed. After lunch, he told the whole class what an awful business decision I had made.

I remember a time in sixth grade when I forgot my homework. I was on the honor roll and I rarely forgot my homework. When the teacher tried to excuse me, some of the other students were jealous of me and complained. They ended up having a mock trial, which I call "The Peanut Butter and Jelly Sandwich Trial." I called it this because they tried to get me in trouble for everything including bringing in a messy peanut butter and jelly sandwich for lunch that day. Two students even got up and claimed they had stolen some cartons of milk from me when it was my week to help sell milk in the cafeteria. They did it to show how incompetent I was. These two students did not get punished at all because they said they put the milk cartons back, which they could not prove. After the trial, I ended up having to write two hundred times, "I will remember my homework from now on."

If anyone was caught doing something for which he or she was suspended or expelled, the school held a special chapel service, which all the classes attended, and made an example of that student. The principal would not only call the student's family, he would also call their church and their job, which sometimes resulted in the student getting fired.

My sister had a friend who became pregnant. The girl was in her senior year. She went to the principal for help. The principal expelled her and would not let her finish her senior year. They then had a special chapel service and told everyone in the whole school about the matter. My mom became angry about the way the school handled that situation, and she allowed me to choose the school I would go to for ninth grade. I decided to go to a public school in Wappingers Falls, New York.

Even in this legalistic environment, the Lord still provided me with a few great friends. These friends were the most generous kids I had ever met.

During this time, if I had not had a personal relationship with Jesus, instead of just religion and laws, I would have turned away from the Lord. I could be upset about all the things that happened to me while I was there. I have decided to forgive them.

What Do You Think

The Lord in his wisdom knew that we would not be able to keep all of His commandments. Luckily, He has provided us with a legal clause that is very important. You can have billions of rules and religious laws but if this important clause is missing, they will fail. This important clause is,

"For God so loved the world that He gave His only begotten son,
That whosover believeth in Him should not perish, but have
Everlasting life.
For God sent not his son into the world to condemn the world; but
That the world through Him might be saved.
He that believeth on Him is not condemned: but he that
Believeth not is condemned already, because He hath
Not believed in the name of the only begotten Son of God."
(John 3: 16-18)

Remember that Jesus did not come into the world to change the laws or do away with them. He came to fulfill them. This passage fulfills the law, because it no longer matters how good we are, how we dress, or what we do that saves us. It is Jesus who saves us.

This clause lightens a huge burden that the rest of the laws place on us. It allows us to come as we are, whether we are dressed in a nice suit or in jeans.

This passage also means that it no longer matters what people say about you, only what the Lord says about you. We are no longer condemned by the law and we are free from its effects. We don't have to have it all together and we can still obtain everlasting life and reward.

We no longer have to look for examples of people who violate the laws, but can now look to an example of what will happen if we follow the laws and remember to believe on the name of Jesus. He is an example of hope, mercy, grace, and love. His example is not based on fear, rejection, jealousy, and hatred.

It is no longer us against the world, but Jesus and us against the world. Having Jesus with us against the world is a lot more comforting.

Challenge

Read Exod. (20: 1-20) and Matt. (22: 34-40). As you read these two passages of scripture, ask yourself what similarities and differences if any are there in the commandments discussed in these two passages. Which passage of commandments do your prefer and why?

LESSON 17

Good People are Going to Hell

"The wicked shall be turned into hell, and all the nations that forget God."
(Psal. 9: 17)

The Lord told us to preach the Gospel to every person, nation, tongue, and creature. However, sometimes we let our own pride, prejudice, and hate toward people keep us from following the Lord's words. Jesus loves those people you label as bad and hopeless as much as He loves you. He desires that all come to Him no matter what they have done.

This next poem is about the story of Jonah. Jonah's prejudice and hatred for the people of Ninevah almost led to those people being in hell for all eternity. As you read this next poem, ask the Lord to show you if there is anyone toward whom you harbor hate.

Poem/Song

Those Big, Mean, Awful, Bad, People
One day the Lord came to Jonah the prophet and spoke.
Jonah listened intently who just awoke.
"Go to Ninevah, Jonah and tell them to repent,"
Jonah, after hearing this, became bent.
Jonah's pride started to say "no."
Jonah then joined along with his solo.

Chorus

Those People are Big.
No No No No.
Those People are Mean.
No No No No.
Just the thought of them, just makes me want to scream.
Oh, I just don't want to go.
Those people are awful.
No No No No
Those people are bad.
No No No No.

Just the thought of them just makes me feel so mad.
Oh, I just don't want to go.
For Ninevah to repent was not Jonah's wish.
So he jumped on a boat, and sailed to Tarshish.
This mission, Jonah thought to himself, I will choose.
He sat there contempt while sailing on that cruise.
Jonah's pride started to say no.
Jonah then joined along with his solo.

Chorus

The Lord caused a huge storm to pop up.
The waves along the boat started to erupt.
All the men on board were in panic and fear.
They prayed to God hoping He would hear.
When they drew lots to see who to blame.
To Jonah the prophet, the lot came.
They asked Jonah what he had done.
He told them how he chose to disobey God and run.
He told them how his pride said "no."
Jonah then told them the story of his solo.

Chorus

Jonah thought these men's lives he could not afford,
So he had the men throw him overboard.
The Lord sent a huge fish or a whale,
To catch Jonah as the men continued to sail.
Jonah prayed while with those fish organs and guts,
Jonah was in one of his bad ruts.
The Lord was faithful and answered his prayers.
The Lord had the whale bring Jonah back because He cares.
To Ninevah again, the Lord told Jonah to go.
Jonah went to Ninevah singing his solo.

Chorus

When Jonah got to Ninevah, He told them the news.
Jonah waited on a mountain to see what they'd choose.
While waiting, the Lord had a vine grow.
So that Jonah could stay as cool as snow.
The people of Ninevah repented and turned around,

So the Lord was gracious and chose to spare that town.
Instead of being joyful and glad,
Jonah turned red and got mad.
God sparing Ninevah, that was not fine.
Jonah cared more about the worm that ate his vine.
Jonah's pride just started to say "no."
Jonah continued once again with a different solo.
Those People are big.
No No No No.
Those People are mean.
No No No No.
The way You forgave them just makes me want to scream.
This is why I didn't want to go.
Those people are awful
No No No No
Those people are bad.
No No No No
Your love and grace for them just makes me feel so mad.
This is why I didn't want to go.
Do not be quick to judge and condemn
Or else to the Lord your own actions may offend.
Remember the grace the Lord has given you.
Thank the Lord for His love that's true.
Look to be merciful as the Lord is for your sin.
Desire that everyone come to know Him.
The Lord honors it when we obey.
Instead of rebelling and running away.
Thank the Lord for all of his grace.
Or like Jonah, you may find yourself in a strange place.
With the ending of this poem, we set sail.
Share the Lord with everyone and tell them His tale.
Tell them how Jesus died on that cross.
So He can cover our sin, so we will not be lost.
Serve the Lord when He puts someone on your heart.
And do not let hate for them draw you apart.
Give that unforgiveness to Him.
Don't let it cause you to sin.

What Do You Think?

Good people are going to hell. Kind people are going to hell with murderers. Caring people are going to hell with rapists. Nice people are going to hell with child molesters. People much kinder and nicer than many Christians are going to hell.

Why do I just go to church and not try to reach these people for the Lord? Why do we sit by and watch our friends and relatives go to hell with criminals and strangers?

We are saved through Jesus Christ who paid the price for our sins. We need nice people in heaven, who feed the poor, visit the elderly, and spend Christmas with orphans.

How can we have fun in heaven without nice people? Jesus does not want bench warmers and pew patrollers in heaven. He wants people who love their neighbors as themselves.

Why do I let my fear of speaking keep me from saving good people from hell? These people are no different from me. I do a lot of good things, yet I was destined for hell because I sin. I thank You, Jesus, for saving my life.

Please save all my friends and family. Reach them for You, Lord. Do not blot their names out of your Book of Life. I realize that I am not the Holy Spirit. Without the Holy Spirit, I will fail by my own flesh.

However, the church needs to wake up. The body of Christ needs to open its eyes and ears. We need to throw the religious laws in the garbage and preach to every nation, tongue, tribe, and family.

Deliver us, oh Lord, from traditionalism and deliver us from hypocrisy. Knock us off those pews and benches. Be with me when I speak Your name and help me to check my pride at the door, because we need good people in heaven.

Challenge

Read through the book of Jonah. Do you have trouble talking about Jesus to someone? Is it because you have unforgiveness or prejudice? Is it because you are afraid?

Ask the Lord for help to forgive anyone or any group of people that may have wronged you in the past. Ask the Lord to also remove any fear of speaking to people or fear of rejection.

The harvest is plentiful but the laborers are few. The Lord is looking for people who will give up their pride, prejudices, and fears to serve Him. Will you be one of them or would you prefer good people in hell?

LESSON 18

Four Hundred-Year Period

"Lord, now lettest thou thy servant depart in peace, according to thy word:
For mine eyes have seen thy salvation," (Luke 2: 29-30)

What Jesus did on the cross for us was a perfect example of His love for us. There is no way we could ever pay back the Lord for what He has done.

This next poem is about the gift Jesus gave us that we can never pay back. Jesus knows that and yet He still loves us.

Poem/Song

Payback
I can't pay Him back!!!
I can't pay Him back!!!
Jesus died on that Cross.
I am at a loss.
How can I possibly pay?
Even if I work everyday.
My sins were such an enormous stack.
I can't pay Him back!!!
I can't pay Him back!!!
No matter how much I try.
No matter how much I cry.
I can't pay my debt
Even if I won every bet.
Betting on races at the track.
I can't pay Him back!!!
I can't pay Him back!!!
I can try harder to be good.
Oh, I only wish I could.
I could give to the poor.
I know that I could give more.
But, no matter how much I pick up the slack.

I can't pay Him back!!!
I can't pay Him back!!!
How in the World can I pay Him back??
Then Jesus showed me this was a gift, not a loan.
He did this because He loves me, my mind is blown.
The only condition of this gift is that you receive.
That Jesus loves you, That's all you have to believe.
This gift was given because he cared.
Just remember this gift should be shared.

What Do You Think?

There is a period of about four hundred years between where the events in the Old Testament end and events in the New Testament begin. Some people call this the **Silent Period**, because there was no record of the Lord doing anything during this time.

What was God doing during this four hundred-year period? Was He sleeping or was He on a four hundred-year vacation?

The Bible says that He will never leave us or forsake us. I don't believe that He was not doing anything during this four hundred year-period. God was preparing for His son Jesus to come into the world in the form of a baby.

When Mary and Joseph brought Jesus into the temple a couple of days after His birth, a man named Simeon was there. The Holy Spirit had revealed to Simeon that he would not die until he saw the Messiah. This shows that the Holy Spirit was present even before He visited the disciples after Jesus ascended into heaven.

The Holy Spirit was around before the world began. In the book of Genesis, it says that the Spirit of the Lord hovered over the waters before the Lord said "Let there be light."

Jesus was also present before the beginning of the world. John Chapter 1 says, "the Word was with God and the Word was God." When the Lord created man, He said "Let us make man in **Our** image." He did not use the word **My**.

The Trinity always existed. Anyone who does not believe in Jesus does not know God the Father.

Jesus was with us before we even knew His name. Jesus knew who we were when He died on that cross.

I assure you that the Lord was not resting during that four hundred-year period. He was working more than ever to make sure the events unfolded perfectly for Jesus, so that He could come into the world to save us from our sins.

Challenge

God works more overtime than anyone. We complain when we have to work an hour of overtime. He works 24/7. He comforts us, protects us, and He even leaves heaven to spend time with us while we are down here on the earth. His idea of vacation is spending time with *us*.

Take some bread and some grape juice and have communion. The bread represents the body of Christ who died for us. The grape juice represents the blood that was shed for us. Take some time right now to thank the Lord for dying on the cross for your sins. Once you have done so, eat the bread and drink the juice.

Grace and peace be multiplied unto you through the knowledge of God,

and of Jesus our Lord,

According as His divine power hath given unto us all things that pertain unto life and godliness,

through the knowledge of Him that hath called us to glory and virtue:

Whereby are given unto us exceeding great and precious promises:

that by these ye might be partakers of the divine nature, having escaped the corruption that is in the world through lust.

And beside this, giving all diligence,

add to your faith virtue; and to virtue knowledge;

And to knowledge temperance;

and to temperance patience; and to patience godliness;

And to godliness brotherly kindness;

and to brotherly kindness charity.

For if these things be in you, and abound,

they make you that ye shall neither be barren nor unfruitful in the knowledge of our Lord Jesus Christ.

(2 Pet. 1: 2-8)

LESSON 19
Appreciate Who the Lord Made you to Be

"That the Gentiles should be fellowheirs, and of the same body, and partakers of his promise in Christ by the gospel: Whereof I was made a minister, according to the gift of the grace of God given unto me by the effectual working of his power." (Ephe. 3: 6- 7)

A lot of people who hear the story of David and Goliath, visualize Goliath as the giant. I have a different perspective on this story.

In my next poem, *David* is the giant, since the Lord was with Him when he went out against Goliath. If the Lord is for us, who can be against us. With Christ, we can be giants also.

Poem/Song

Heart of a Giant
In the book of I Samuel chapter seventeen.
There is a battle between Israel and the Philistine.
From the Philistine army, a man stepped out of rank.
This man was huge and built like a tank.
This man was an enormous pile of mass.
He was a giant covered head to toe in brass.
Goliath was this giant's name.
He challenged Israel to a little game.
He boasted with a smile and a grin.
If any man would fight him and win.
The Philistines would be Israel's servants.
But if He wins, Israel would have to hide like hermits.
For forty days he defied the Jews.
They were frightened constantly by this news.
One day a boy named David came with supplies.
Just in time to hear Goliath's replies.
David's face turned beat red.
David sang to the people as he said,

Chorus

Fi, Fi, Fo, Fo, Fum, Fe.
God will deliver him over to me.
Fo, Fo, Fum, Fum, Fe, Fi.
For this sin, this giant will die.
Fum, Fum, Fe, Fe, Fi, Fo.
God will end this with just one blow.
Fe, Fe, Fi, Fi, Fo, Fum
I come in the name of God and Son.
Fe, Fe, Fi, Fi, Fo, Fum
Ready or Not, Here I come.
After hearing this disturbing tune.
Eliab, David's brother came with gloom.
Jealous that David was anointed next as king,
Out of his mouth, insults started to fling.
Other people thought David was a joke.
David sang to the people as he spoke.

Chorus

When Saul heard about David, He had instant joy.
But when he met David, he saw just a boy.
Saul didn't think this fight would be fair.
But David told him how he killed the lion and bear.
"This Philistine giant is one of them," David squawked.
David sang to the people as he talked.

Chorus

Saul gave David his armor to get in the groove.
But once the armor was on, David couldn't move.
So David took it off and took up his staff.
Along with five stones, a sling, and a laugh.
When Goliath saw David, he wasn't benign.
Because he thought he was being treated as a canine.
So they shared with each other some very harsh words.
They threatened to throw each other's flesh to the birds.
David said he would cut Goliath's head off where it lay.
David then sang to the Lord as he started to pray.
Fi, Fi, Fo, Fo, Fum, Fe.
You will deliver him over to me.
Fo, Fo, Fum, Fum, Fe, Fi.
For this sin, this giant will die.

Fum, Fum, Fe, Fe, Fi, Fo.
You will end this with just one blow.
Fe, Fe, Fi, Fi, Fo, Fum
I come in your name dear God and Son.
Fe, Fe, Fi, Fi, Fo, Fum
Ready or not, here I come.
David got up and to Goliath he ran.
God gave him more courage than any man.
David then took his sling.
And with one rock, let it fling.
The rock struck the giant in the head.
Goliath's body dropped and lay dead.
The other Philistines turned and fled.
David sang to the Lord as he said,
FI, FI, Fo, Fo, Fum, Fe.
You have deliver him over to me.
Fo, Fo, Fum, Fum, Fe, Fi.
If any defy, they will die.
Fum, Fum, Fe, Fe, Fi, Fo.
You have ended this with just one blow.
Fe, Fe, Fi, Fi, Fo, Fum
I come in your name dear God and Son.
Fe, Fe, Fi, Fi, Fo, Fum
Ready or not, here I come.

Life Experience

I went to Roy C. Ketcham high school in Wappingers Falls, New York. When I got into high school, I found that overall kids were a lot nicer than at the private Christian school I had come from. One kid called me names when I first started. I just ignored it and didn't say anything to him. Eventually he stopped calling me names and his whole attitude changed. I continued to improve academically.

However, while school was better, things in my neighborhood got worse. The father of one of my best friends got transferred to a church in Pennsylvania and they had to move away. Another friend of mine started hanging out with some kids in my neighborhood who were having some issues.

I was worried about my friend. I wanted to be there for him as he had been there for me. I just didn't know what to do. It is tough when you see people you love in trouble and you can't lift a finger to help them.

I thank the Lord that I had a bike, because I spent a lot of my time exploring new roads and trails just to cope with my anger and worrying.

Back then, I hated who I was. I was also very angry with the world. I just wanted things to change. After I failed my first driving test, I felt very discouraged, angry, and alone. I tried to turn to humor to cope with everything by telling everyone stories about Communists and dragons. I guess I imagined myself as some kind of secret agent or dragon warrior.

So, I started telling these stories about Communist plots and dragons. One story was about operation P. O. P. It stood for Piss On People. It was a plan where the Communists would seed the clouds with something that would make everyone who was exposed to it instantly have to run to the bathroom. While everyone would fight to get into a bathroom, the Communists would take over the world.

I also talked about different kinds of dragons. It was almost like Pokemon. One dragon looked like a car and another one looked like a girl with a blue dotted tongue.

While everyone was laughing with me or at me on the outside, I was dying on the inside. At the time, my mom was going to a church across the river in Kingston, New York. It was a Messianic Jewish church. There were services on Saturday and Sunday. I decided to go with my mom to this church.

At this church, the Holy Ghost really showed up at the meetings and everyone was on the floor. It was a place I could go to relax and give my burdens to Him. I remember it was prophesied at one service that I was a "mighty firefighter", and that I would go wherever the Devil stirred up fires and put out those flames.

These meetings really helped me. The Lord helped me like who I was in Him. Before, I would try to pretend to be different people, like one of my friends or someone cool just to try and get people to like me. No matter how much you try to be like someone else, you will never be that person. You have to love who the Lord made you to be and use your talents to glorify Him if you want the most benefit from your life.

Once I loved who the Lord made me to be, I stopped pretending to be other people and I started taking control of my life. I decided to get a part-time job. I got my first job at Kmart. I worked at Kmart right through college. It was a steady job with a steady income to pay my tuition for college and my car expenses.

I continued to pray for my friend. The Lord answered my prayers.

I went to Brown's Driving school, and I passed my second driving test. I graduated from high school in the summer of 1997.

Challenge

David had a lot of opposition against Him when He went to step out for the Lord. Read I Samuel chapter 17. Was there ever a time when the Lord called you to do something and as soon as you went to do it, someone or something started to come against you in order to talk you out of it?

The Lord has called each of us with a unique plan and purpose for our lives. He has plans to help us and not to harm us. Ask the Lord to reveal to you what His plan for your life is.

LESSON 20
The Person in the Mirror

"As ye know how we exhorted and comforted and charged every one of you, as a father doth his children, That ye would walk worthy of God, who hath called you unto his kingdom and glory." (I Thes. 2: 11-12)

The Lord is not just a God that you worship when you're happy and everything is all right. He is a God who is there for you even in your trials and tribulations. A lot of times, when we feel alone, sad, mad, or fearful we don't always think about worshipping the Lord. This is what we should do when we get these very feelings.

Sometimes we get this idea that we always have to have it all together and think happy thoughts when we worship God. The problem is that we don't. However, we serve a God who cares about how we feel and is not offended or upset with us when we get upset, hopeless, and depressed.

This next song was written to encourage you to talk to the Lord when you are down and tell Him your concerns. He is always there to listen.

Poem/Song

Carry Me

Verse 1
When I am all alone and people leave me off for dead.
I will open up my heart. I will lift my weary head.
And I will get down on my knees.
Because I know!
that Jesus Christ hears me.

Chorus

Carry me through my troubles,
Carry me through the valleys,
Carry me over the mountains,

Carry me through the oceans,
Carry me through the seas.
Help me to become all that you
Made me to be!
Verse 2
When I can't go on no more,
And life will not let me soar,
Like an eagle in the sky,
And I am just ready to cry,
I get down on my knees,
Because I know
That Jesus Christ hears me

Chorus

Verse 3
When I keep on asking Why?
And I am reminded that I'll die, Or I really hate that guy
Or girl.
When I'm so angry with the world,
I get down on my knees
Because I know
That Jesus Christ hears me!

Chorus

What Do You Think?

The Lord has forgiven us. However, sometimes we do not forgive all our enemies. Sometimes the hardest person to forgive is in the mirror.

We must love who the Lord has created us to be. Stop pretending to be someone the Lord has not made you to be. The Lord knows your weaknesses and strengths. Sometimes we focus so much on changing our weaknesses that we forget the gifts the Lord has given us.

We all make mistakes. The Lord is perfect. The only thing that we can show perfectly is His love. Whether it is just one sin or a thousand, the Lord shows His grace and mercy to those who turn back to Him.

Help me to stay in Your presence and not try to be someone that I'm not. I am a child of the King. He will help me to overcome things at work, on the road, and around the house.

We must forgive ourselves just as the Lord has forgiven us.

Challenge

Is there a situation that you are currently struggling with but are afraid to talk to the Lord about? Are you questioning what God is doing concerning a situation and you don't seem to be getting an answer?

Is there something that you want to tell the Lord but you are afraid to say? Remember, the Lord knows everything about us. He is the one who created you. He knows what we are doing all the time. He knows what we are thinking.

Find a quiet place and really get into the Lord's presence. Tell Him truthfully how you feel even though it may not be the most pleasant thing to say. Don't hold back your feelings.

But the Lord shall endure for ever:

He hath prepared His throne for judgment.

And He shall judge the world in righteousness,

He shall minister judgment to the people in uprightness.

The Lord also will be a refuge for the oppressed,

a refuge in times of trouble.

And they that know thy name will put their trust in thee:

for thou, Lord, hast not forsaken them that seek thee.

(Psal. 9: 7-10)

LESSON 21
What Do I Want to Do for a Living?

"Now therefore fear the Lord, and serve him in sincerity and in truth: and put away the gods which your fathers served on the other side of the flood, and in Egypt; and serve ye the Lord." (Josh. 24:14)

Sometimes we wonder why we go through trials. Sometimes it is because we have sinned. Other times it is because the Devil is attacking us. Then again, it could be just the fragile world we live in. Or is it the Lord speaking to us?

All of us go through struggles in this life. Know that all things work together for good. Keep praying and trusting in the Lord, knowing that He will deliver you from your circumstances.

This next poem is about the story of Joseph. Joseph had to go through a lot of trials that he could not understand. Even though things seemed bleak, Joseph still trusted in the Lord. Because of His trust in the Lord, He ended up being second in command in Egypt next to Pharaoh and saving his family from dying of starvation.

Poem/Song

A Question to Ponder Sometimes
Once, there was a man named Jacob who had twelve sons.
He had one son name Joseph who he loved tons.
Jacob gave Joseph a multicolored coat.
This gave the other brothers a sour note.
They planned on killing their brother.
Because they were jealous like no other.
One day they grabbed him and threw him into a pit.
What to do with him, they plan as they sit.
Some Ishmaelites just happened to pass by.
So they sold Joseph as a slave and said bye-bye.
They took Joseph's coat.
And dipped it in the blood of a goat.
They told his father that he had been eaten.

Meanwhile, Joseph felt lost and beaten.
Joseph was stunned and had doubt.
This question as a song was bellowed out,

Chorus

Ding a Ling a Ling a Ling a Ling
Ding a Ling a Ling a Ling a Ling
Here's a question I just gotta sing.
Why do we go through such awful things?
Even when we serve the King of Kings.
I thought we didn't have to worry about a thing.
Ding a Ling a Ling a Ling a Ling
Ding a Ling a Ling a Ling a Ling
Joseph was brought to Egypt, which was pretty far.
He was sold as a slave to Potiphar.
Potiphar was one of Pharoah's top men.
He made Joseph in charge of his den.
The Lord gave Joseph favor in his sight,
Because Joseph continued to do what was right
However, all this impressed Potiphar's spouse.
She turned out to be a real louse.
Day after day, she asked Joseph to come to bed.
This gave Joseph something to dread.
One day, she grabbed Joseph like a varmint.
Joseph ran and left without his garment.
Potiphar's wife got really mad.
She accused Joseph of being bad.
Potiphar threw Joseph in jail.
This caused Joseph to really sing and wail.

Chorus

Even though life in prison was really hard.
The Lord gave Joseph favor with the guard.
He put Joseph in charge of all.
The guard didn't even bother to check on him or call.
Because the guard knew the Joseph was a great guy,
the guard knew that Joseph would not tell a lie.
One day Joseph met a butler and a baker.
They were sent there by Pharaoh to meet their Maker.
They both had weird dreams which left them unrest,

So Joseph interpreted those dreams to the very best.
The baker would die, the butler would be restored.
Joseph told the butler, who would be adored,
"Remember to mention me when you get out."
But the butler forgot, this caused Joseph to pout.
Joseph looked up to Heaven to see.
A question he sang was how could this be?

Chorus

Two years later, Pharaoh was in distress.
He had a dream about cattle and corn to address.
He asked if the magicians could shine some light.
But there comprehension was unclear as the darkness of night.
The butler remembered Joseph in jail.
Pharaoh ordered the guard to get Joseph and sail. the dreams told of seven
years of plenty and famine.
This gave the Pharaoh rest who was jammin. So he set up Joseph as second
in command.
Who would collect good food for Pharaoh's demand.
So the years of plenty came and went. So to Egypt Jacob's sons were sent.
When Joseph saw them, he played a prank.
He pretended he didn't know them when he would fill up their tank.
He would accuse his brothers as spies.
He really gave it to those guys.
Eventually, he caved in.
He told them to move to Egypt and stay with him.
Joseph saw the Lord's plan unfold.
This song in his heart came as it told
Ding a Ling a Ling a Ling a Ling
Ding a Ling a Ling a Ling a Ling
Thank you God the King of Kings.
You answered the question that I sing.
Sometimes we go through such awful things,
But trust the Lord who knows everything.
Ding a Ling a Ling a Ling a Ling
Ding a Ling a Ling a Ling a Ling

Life Experience

I had no idea what I wanted to do when I got to college. A lot of people said that I should go for engineering. I didn't really know what an engineer did. All I knew was that it didn't mean driving a train.

I went to Dutchess Community college in Poughkeepsie, New York. College was a lot different from high school. There were more chapters to read and a different schedule every day. I continued to work part-time at Kmart.

I went for engineering. The curriculum required a lot of credits per semester. I had to buy special tools, such as a compass, drawing triangles, and special drawing paper. I think I only used them for one homework assignment and that was it.

The rest of the assignments were done using a computer program called AutoCad. AutoCad was a terrible program to work with. No matter what computer I was on, the program always seemed to die on me when I was right in the middle of completing a project. I would have to redo each assignment five or six times. I saved them on disks, but even then the files wouldn't work or I couldn't access the data on the files after problems occurred with the program.

I started wondering if I should continue studying engineering. I prayed to the Lord for direction.

For the second semester, I decided to take mostly classes that would apply to any curriculum. I also took a computer science class in C++, since the curriculum was so similar to engineering. At first I really struggled in this class. I was the last person in the computer lab to complete a project. Eventually, I got better at it. I even constructed a giant menu that could do different programs. One of the programs was a watchdog function in which you could record the current time and then select a number of minutes in the future. The program would then tell you the time that many minutes later. I liked it as a hobby, but I didn't see myself doing this for a living.

For the third semester, I decided to go for accounting, since my dad is an accountant. The classes were great, and I took to them like a duck to water. I felt this was the direction the Lord had me going in. I got my Associate's Degree in Business Administration and transferred my credits to a State University of New York (SUNY) in New Paltz, New York.

I never took out any loans for college. I commuted to and from the college. My parents did not pay my tuition or the insurance on my car. The Lord always provided me with the funds I needed.

Challenge

Are you struggling with what to do next? Are you currently asking the Lord for guidance?

Read the story of Joseph in Genesis Chapter 37 and Genesis chapters 39 to 50. Joseph trusted in the Lord and eventually He became second in command to Pharaoh. Joseph realized that He was going through training in order to prepare Him for the position ahead. Ask the Lord to prepare you for the destiny He has for you.

LESSON 22
The Crossing

"Enter into his gates with thanksgiving, and into his courts with praise: be thankful unto him, and bless his name." (Psal. 100:4)

We have so much to be thankful for. It is always important to give thanks to the Lord. Ask the Lord into your day. He is there twenty four hours a day. He will never leave you or forsake you.

This next poem describes different things to be thankful for throughout your day. Take the time to give Him thanks.

Poem/Song

Praise Around the Clock
As the hands go ticking around the clock
The sound of your heart is going tick tock.
Remember to praise the Lord for all he has done.
He sent from Heaven His glorious Son.
When I wake up, the small hand is on seven
I thank the Lord that I am going to Heaven.
He sent his Son to die on the cross
So that my soul would not be lost.
When the small hand is on eight.
I thank the Lord for His words that set me straight.
They guide me through the day to do what's right,
Because we are all precious in his sight.
When the small hand is on nine.
I thank the Lord that my health is fine.
I am not sick and my body is intact.
Jesus has healed me and that is a fact.
When the small hand is on ten.
I thank the Lord for saving me again.
It is His grace that I need.
It is not by my might that I will succeed.
When the small hand is on eleven.

I thank the Lord for a 7/11.
Thank you Lord for places to shop.
I can get plenty of clothes and food with one stop.
When the small hand is on twelve noon.
Remember that Jesus is coming soon.
Don't spend your life collecting material things.
Build up treasures in Heaven, like seeing angel's wings.
When the small hand is on one.
Thank the Lord for everything that's fun.
Family, friends, pets, parties, and sports;
these things are provided as Heaven's exports.
When the small hand is on two.
Think about how much Jesus loves you.
He loves you more than you can ever know.
You are a star on his never ending show.
When the small hand is on three.
Thank the Lord for everything seen and unseen.
Thank Him for everything small and great.
From things that are early to things that are late.
When the small hand is on four.
Get into the Lord's presence on the floor.
Lay down in his peace, love, and joy.
His spirit is there anytime to enjoy.
When the small hand is on five.
Thank the Lord that you are still alive.
Work is done. Time to go home.
Spend time with the family, not on the phone.
When the small hand is on six.
Thank the Lord again just for kicks.
Thank Him for the dinner on your table.
Thank Him for your water, electricity, and cable.
Into the evening, continue to worship and praise.
Thank the Lord all of your days.
Praise him into the darkness of the night.
Then be quiet and listen till the morning's light.
As the world keeps spinning round and round.
Remember the Lord, make a joyful sound.
Another day to bring Him your thanks.
It's more valuable than gold in all the banks.

Life Experience

I continued my classes at the SUNY in New Paltz, New York for my Bachelor of Science degree in accounting. I graduated in December 2001.

I still worked at Kmart and the Lord continued to provide me with funds for my tuition, insurance on my car, gas, and other expenses. I never had to take out a student loan for college.

During this time, the Lord did some great things in my life. My parents and I started to go to Faith Assembly of God church in Poughkeepsie New York. The great thing about this church was that they had a group called The Crossing, for single young adults.

I decided to give it a try. I met a very nice girl there who ran the group at the time. The Crossing was a great place, where believers could get together and worship the Lord, study the Bible, and fellowship with other believers in Christ. It was a big group, and there were fifteen to twenty people in the group at the time. We would go out to eat, see movies, and do things together.

I loved the way everyone was so accepting of people when they walked in for the first time. It was such a blessing having friends who loved Jesus as much as I did.

It is now currently run by a pastor who is a very kind wise man.

Another way the Lord blessed me during this time was to deliver my dad from heavy drinking. He no longer drank alcoholic beverages and he spent more time with my mom, my sister, and me on a regular basis.

Don't ever give up on praying for people. You may not see an answer right away but the Lord will answer you.

Challenge

The Lord is faithful in so many ways. If you have a place to live, count yourself blessed. If you have friends and family that love you, count yourself blessed. The Lord does not stop being faithful. He is faithful and He never has to take a break.

Reflect on the past week and ask the Lord to show you all the things to be thankful for. You may want to write a list.

Have you done this already but still have not noticed any changes? The Lord is still working whether we see Him or not. We just have to keep trusting Him. This is not an easy task. Pray to the Lord to give you perseverance to get through your trials throughout the day.

It is of the Lord's mercies that we are not consumed,

> *because His compassions fail not.*

They are new every morning:

> *great is thy faithfulness.*

The Lord is my portion, saith my soul;

> *therefore will I hope in Him.*

The Lord is good unto them that wait for Him,

> *to the soul that seeketh Him.*

It is good that a man should both hope and quietly wait for the salvation of the Lord.

(Lam. 3: 22-26)

LESSON 23
I Need a Quick Fix

"To every thing there is a season, and a time to every purpose
under the heaven:" (Eccl. 3:1)

We all want to hear the Lord's voice in our lives. Unfortunately, a lot of us don't take the time or don't have the time to stop and listen to His still small voice. Sometimes it is hard to concentrate on Him with all the noise in the world.

This next poem was written to encourage you to take the time to listen to Him. How can we know what His will is for our lives if we do not take the time to listen for His still small voice.

Poem/Song

The Voice
If I could only make one more choice,
It would be to hear the still low sound of your voice.
Just to hear you call my name,
No other sound would be the same.
Every word that you speak
flows to my heart like a gentle creek.
When you open up your mouth and talk
To infinity will I go and walk.
Every word that you whisper
Burns deep in my heart with every flicker.
You never raise your voice and shout,
Unless it is to remove fear and doubt.
Every note that you perfectly sing
Echoes through my ears as a ring.
Every chorus you delightfully hum
Makes me dance like a beat to a drum.
I want to hear each word very clear.
Help me Lord to open up my ear.
Help me to listen for your voice when I pray,
Because I want to hear clearly what you say.

What Do You Think?

Time is so short. There is so much I want to do. Time cannot be bought with money. Time cannot be replaced. When we get to heaven, there will not be any time. That is a hard concept to grasp.

Sometimes we ask the Lord for direction, but we don't stick around to hear His direction. We try to set up fleeces like Gideon did in the book of Judges so that we can get a quick answer or get out of talking with God. We may ask Him, "Lord if it is meant for me to do this let it rain," or "If it is sunny, I will do that." Sometimes we flip a coin or we roll dice to decide which choice we should make.

Sometimes you have to make a quick decision and it is not always easy to wait upon the Lord. However, when He does show us which way to go, it is well worth the wait. It is better to be in His presence and follow His course than to make up our own course and fail or end up walking around in circles.

We need to forget the fleeces and pray to the Lord expecting a direct answer. This is an area that I really struggle with. I like a quick fix to the problems that I have.

Help me, Lord, to stand on Your commandments and to be in Your will. Help me not to look at what a coin, dice, the weather, or other people tell me to do but to look directly at You.

Challenge

Do you take the time to listen to the Lord? Do you do all the talking when you pray or do you give the Lord time to reply?

Ask the Lord to speak to you. Take some time to just be quiet before the Lord and find out what He has to say. Remember not to rush Him.

LESSON 24

When There is No Answer

"Lead me in thy truth, and teach me: for thou art the God of my salvation;
on thee do I wait all the day." (Psal. 25: 5)

Sometimes we do not understand the Lord's plan. We wonder why we are going through things and we don't seem to be getting an answer. Continue to press into the Lord and trust Him during these times in your life.

This next poem is about the story of Job. Job was a man of God who waited upon the Lord even when things got worse. Sometimes we must lose everything in order to gain more of Him. However, once you gain more of Him, you will be more blessed than you were before. Remember one blessing is worth more than all the money in the world.

Poem/Song

Job's Blue Song
One day up in Heaven, God's home,
Satan came before God's throne.
The Lord said, "look at my servant, Job.
There is no one like him on all the globe."
Satan replied, "this man is calling your bluff.
Job just loves you because of all his stuff."
So the Lord allowed Satan to take it all away.
So Satan went out to give Job a very bad day.
Satan took away his oxen, camels, donkeys, and sheep.
This was a loss for Job that was really deep.
Job didn't even have a second to catch his mouth that fell,
But he found out that his children had died as well.
Puzzled, from this unpleasant ride,
Job sang this song as he cried.

Chorus

Dum Dum De Dum Dum Di
Why me, I'm just a simple guy.
As I lay here, I cry and mourn.
I wish I was never ever born.
I wonder if I did sin.
But if He slay me, I will trust Him.
But what's up, please tell me why.
Dum Dum De Dum Dum Di.
As we read this next part of this poem,
We see Satan standing again at God's throne.
The Lord said, "In all that you did, Job did not sin.
You have taken everything from him, even his next of kin."
Satan then replied, "It's no problem giving up his wealth.
Job just saved himself to promote his health."
So the Lord gave him permission to launch attacks and spoils,
Satan attacked Job's health by inflicting him with boils.
To this, Job just replied,
And sang this song as he cried.

Chorus

So people looked at Job in a different tone.
Never in all his life had Job felt so alone.
His wife told Job to curse God and be dead.
And she left him sick as a dog in bed.
Also to all the people in the town,
Job became to them as Bozo the Clown.
To Job's servants he was one to be despised,
So Job sang this song as he cried,

Chorus

Because back then, they didn't have a phone,
Job's three friends came who were bad to the bone.
Eliphaz the Temanite, Bildad the Shuhite, and Zophar
They showed up at Job's house from afar.
They thought because of this Job had done something wrong.
Their questions and taunts came upon Job very strong.
As their accusations just punched and jibed.
Job sang this song as he cried,

Chorus

Finally God came down into their zone.
God spoke up and made his voice known.
Where were you when I made the world?
Like the behemoth, I'll give you a twirl.
Don't think you're so righteous. Don't be quick to judge.
God told the three friends to stop treating Job as sludge.
Remember, before you move the splinter, move your own plank.
When bad things happen to people, help and don't quickly spank.
Don't judge others. It's up to Him to decide.
So job sang with joy as he cried,
Dum Dum De Dum Dum Di
Why me, I'm just a lucky guy.
I say that He will always restore.
He has blessed me more than before.
I no longer try to work off my sin.
Even when you're slain, still trust him.
Now it is time to say goodbye.
Dum Dum De Dum Dum Di.

What Do You Think?

One night at The Crossing, a friend of mine told me that he was asking the Lord a question. He said he was fasting and praying to the Lord but was not getting a response. He said that plenty of other people were giving him advice on a million different things for him to do when he prayed or fasted. He tried them, but he said that he still did not receive an answer from the Lord concerning his question.

I admire this friend. He has such a passion and love for the Lord. I wish I had the love for the Lord that this friend has for Him. I also admire how he dedicates his time and has a hunger to just hear from the Lord. I know in time the Lord will answer his question and he will be satisfied.

I myself have never fasted. I have prayed small prayers throughout the day. I pray to Him in the mornings during my hour and fifteen minute commute to work. The Lord has revealed things to me. Maybe if I fasted, I would more clearly hear Him.

A lot of times, you pray and go into the presence of the Lord and you go away feeling great. Other times you pray or have people pray over you and you leave feeling empty. In these situations, where we are seeking Him for answers, we feel discouraged and abandoned. We wonder what we are doing wrong.

Sometimes people think that when things don't go according to plan, a person must be doing something wrong or in some kind of sin. We need to put away the sin in our lives.

However, this may not always be the case. Remember how Job did not sin, yet lost his family, possessions, and a lot of close friends.

Sometimes people simply say, in these situations, that they just need to pray more or they just need to fast more. Sometimes we spend so much time worrying about the details involved with fasting and praying correctly that we lose sight of why we are praying or fasting to the Lord in the first place.

Are we just praying to get an answer from the Lord so that we don't have to keep praying and fasting, or are we seeking Him because we love Him and desire His plan for our lives?

Are we looking at the clock trying to force God to answer us in a specific amount of time like a five minute, twenty-minute, one-hour, ten-hour, or forty-day period? Are we doing all the talking when we pray or are we giving God a chance to speak? Are we truly open to what He is telling us to do or are we too busy with other things that He has not called us to do? Do we really want to know what God is directing us to do or are we dismissing it because it doesn't sound like fun? Do we know but just don't feel like doing it?

Challenge

I am not going to tell you to fast or pray twenty-three hours a day. It is not always about quantity but about quality when it comes to spending time with someone. The Lord made us all unique, with a special plan only we can carry out. He gave us different talents, skills, and ways to seek Him and get closer to Him.

Remember how Jacob had to wrestle with God to get a blessing from Him. Remember that Abraham, while he was on the earth, never saw all the generations of people as numerous as the grains of sand on the seashore yet he trusted in the Lord. Joseph was in prison in Egypt for a long time before the Lord took him out of that place and made him second to Pharaoh? Moses was up on top of Mount Sinai for forty days before he received the Ten Commandments.

Just love Him and spend time with Him. It is great to bring your questions to Him, but don't let them rob you of the joy He gives you. The Lord is bigger than any question or concern and He will take care of them. Is there a question that the Almighty God does not know the answer to?

> *Reflect on the story of Job. As you read this, think of someone who is currently going through a trial. Why do you think they are going through it? Do you think that it is because they did something to displease God? Ask the Lord to show you if you have been judging people unfairly when they are going through any trials and ask the Lord for repentance.*

Trust in the Lord with all thine heart;

and lean not unto thine own understanding.

In all thy ways acknowledge him,

and he shall direct thy paths.

Be not wise in thine own eyes:

fear the Lord, and depart from evil.

It shall be health to thy navel,

and marrow to thy bones.

(Prov. 3: 5-8)

LESSON 25

The MBA Decision

"Ask and it shall be given you; seek, and ye shall find; knock, and it shall
be opened unto you:" (Matt. 7:7)

In this life, our faith will be tested from time to time. We need to remember to stay focused on Him when we are pressured to compromise our devotion to Him for immediate gratification.

This next poem is about Shadrach, Meshach, and Abednego. They had to make a choice on whether to stand by their faith in the Lord or save their lives. No matter what happens in this life, it is worth nothing compared to what happens in the next.

Poem/Song

Charcoal

NARRATOR

In the City of Babylon, Nebuchadnezzer was king.
He created an image of gold, It was a remarkable thing.
The image was three score cubits high.
The depth was six cubits and stretched towards the sky.
The king called all that were in charge.
To dedicate the statue which was very large.
At the dedication there were sounds of cornets, harps, and flutes.
There were sackbuts, psalteries, dulcimers and toots.
A herald ordered by the king.
Got up and started to sing.
Do Do Do Do Do
Do Do Do Do Do

Herald

When you hear the funky beat.
Drop down to your feet.
If you don't bow where you seat.
We'll turn up the heat.
in the furnace it's not sweet.

And it isn't very neat. So don't try to cheat.
To the ground your head must meet.
Do Do Do Do Do
Do Do Do Do Do

Narrator

So everyone in the city started to bow.
But there were three who questioned how.
They were Shadrach, Meshach, and Abednego.
To the king, they were ordered to go.
Once they were before the king.
The king got up and started to sing.
Do Do Do Do Do
Do Do Do Do Do

King Nebuchadnezzar

You didn't bow, please tell me why
Oh, maybe you didn't hear the herald cry.
I'll give you one more chance right now.
To the image of gold you must surely bow.
If you don't bow to the image of gold.
You'll be thrown in the furnace and become charcoal.
Do Do Do Do Do
Do Do Do Do Do

Narrator

Shadrach, Meshach, and Abednego stood their ground.
They trusted in the Lord who is always around.
They didn't wimper, scream, or cry.
To the king they boldly sang their reply.
Do Do Do Do Do
Do Do Do Do Do

Shadrack, Meshack & Abednego

In the name of the Lord, we must take a stand.
He is able to deliver us from out of your hand.
But even if we die for this enterprise,
We will not bow down or even compromise.
To the Lord we remain faithful and bold.
So we must say no to the image of gold.
Do Do Do Do Do
Do Do Do Do Do

Narrator

King Nebuchadnezzer was full of rage.
He called his men up to the stage.
He told them to make the furnace seven times as hot.
Shadrach, Meshack, and Abednego were on the spot.
Their reply really angered the king.
The king got up and to the men began to sing.
Do Do Do Do Do
Do Do Do Do Do

King Nebuchadnezzer

What you gonna do when the fire engulfs you?
It will burn your flesh, your bones will be consumed.
Because you won't bow to the image of gold,
Your body and soul will become charcoal.
Do Do Do Do Do
Do Do Do Do Do

Narrator

So the men were bound and thrown in the fire.
They were thrown in with their fancy clothes and attire.
King Nebuchadnezzer looked puzzled as could be.
He asked "Why are there four? I thought there were three."
The fourth one shone as bright as the sun.
The fourth person in the furnace was God the Son.
So the king called the men out.
And made a decree to sing and shout.
Do Do Do Do Do
Do Do Do Do Do

King Nebuchadnezzer

The Lord protected them from the heat,
So I gotta change the beat.
Because their God is true.
A decree I say to you.
Anyone who speaks against the Lord.
Will be cut in pieces and served on a board.
There house will also be made a dunghill.
Now let's all celebrate and take a chill pill.
Do Do Do Do Do
Do Do Do Do Do

Narrator

The moral of the story is when the world turns up the heat.
Trust in the Lord when you are put in the hot seat.
The world will do anything to pressure you
To defy the Lord who still remains true.
Don't be quick to compromise.
Fear the Lord more. It is considered wise.
This goes out all across our land.
Don't keep quiet. For the Lord, take a stand.
Do Do Do Do Do
Do Do Do Do Do

Life Experience

I continued going to the SUNY in New Paltz, New York, for my Masters of Business Administration (MBA) degree in accounting since they would waive the first twenty-one credits if I went for my MBA right away. I only went part-time, since I really wanted to get a position in accounting.

I tried to pass the Certified Public Accountant (CPA) Exam a couple of times. There were four parts to the exam when it was a written exam: Business Law & Environment, Auditing, FARE, and ARE. The FARE section of the exam dealt with financial accounting for for-profit businesses. The ARE section of the exam dealt with tax accounting, government accounting, non-profit businesses, and cost accounting. Now the exam is done on a computer and the names of the four sections have changed.

I managed to pass the ARE and the FARE sections but I never passed the other two. I feel that the Auditing section of the exam is the toughest section to pass since you have to know the details of each type of audit and the types of reports they do inside and out. I remember another person taking the exam with me who was already an auditor, and even she was stumped.

I didn't feel motivated by the Lord to continue studying for the CPA exam at that time to pass the other two sections. My main focus was to get my MBA degree.

When I got my BS in accounting, I thought that I would surely get a job in accounting. I didn't get hired right away since I still didn't have any experience. I was starting to feel that I'd made a mistake in going for my MBA.

I prayed to the Lord to see if I should continue to get my MBA degree. I remember the next morning waking up and having such a supernatural peace about things. It was the kind of peace that allows lambs to sleep with lions without fear of being harmed. So I kept at it.

Challenge

When the Lord tells you to do something, He will always be there for you, even in your trials.

Read Daniel Chapter 3. As you read this passage, think about your life. Is there something that is stopping you from remaining faithful to Him when you are confronted by the culture or other people? Are you willing to give your life for the Lord?

Ask the Lord for boldness and zeal for Him. Ask the Lord to help you not to compromise your faith. Remember He that is in you is greater than he that is in the world.

LESSON 26
Where are Your Credentials?

"Who is wise, and he shall understand these things? prudent, and he shall know them? for the ways of the Lord are right, and the just shall walk in them: but the transgressors shall fall therein." (Hosea 14: 9)

Jealousy and envy are very deadly sins in the body of Christ. There is too much competitiveness in the churches. People are so busy coveting other people's gifts, that they miss out on the gifts the Lord has given them. The Devil wants you to focus on your weaknesses and the strengths of others instead of focusing on the strengths the Lord has given you.

This next poem is the story of Daniel and the lions den. As one can see from this story, Jealousy and envy are sins that can lead to murder.

Poem/Song

Cat Food

There once was a man named Daniel the Jew.
His walk with the Lord was mighty and true.
King Darius was the king of Babylon at this time.
Next to the king, Daniel was second in line.
The other presidents, princes, congress and governors
Towards Daniel became jealous men and coveters.
They all got together one night to scam.
The outcome was a devilish plan.
We cannot find fault with this man.
But maybe with his God we can.
We will make it illegal to pray to anyone or anything.
Except to whoever is on the throne serving as king.
With this, the men got up to sing.
Bom Bom Bom

Chorus

What you gonna do when those lions come for you.
They will eat your flesh. Your bones will be chewed.
No god whatsoever will be able to save you.
The Daniel you knew will become cat food.
The wicked members went to the king with their decree.
With intent to turn Daniel's body into debris.
When the king heard it, he was tickled pink.
"What a great decree!" he started to think.
He sealed and signed the decree with his ring.
With this, the men got up to sing.
Bom Bom Bom

Chorus

When Daniel heard, He was not dismayed.
Night and day, He continued to pray.
Because He didn't care what others could do.
His faith in the Lord just blossomed and grew.
Everything went according to plan.
They caught Daniel praying on a stand.
They cuffed him with chains that started to cling.
With this, the men got up to sing.
Bom Bom Bom

Chorus

When the king found out, he became grieved.
How could He with those men be so deceived.
Nevertheless the damage was done.
Daniel was to die. The men thought they won.
They threw Daniel into that lion's den.
They thought their plan had come to an end.
The mourning bells tolled with a bing.
With this, the men got up to sing.
Bom Bom Bom

Chorus

Next morning, the king got up to see what of Daniel was left.
Running to the lion's den, he mourned and wept.
When he got there, he was stunned and surprised.
To see Daniel and the lions had compromised.

Daniel was untouched and unharmed.
He ordered the men to grab Daniel by the arms.
Get those men who were so zealous
Tried to kill Daniel because they were jealous.
Throw them in the pit and we will see
If unharmed they will also be.
The lions' tails started to swing.
With a different chorus the lions got up to sing.
Bom Bom Bom
What you gonna do when we come for you.
We will eat your flesh. Your bones will be chewed.
Only one God in Heaven could have saved you.
Your jealousy made Him blue. So now you're cat food.
Bom Bom Bom

What Do You Think

In some churches, everyone is treated equally. In other churches, people are not always treated fairly.

Some churches are run by a small minority who do not want to share their power with others in the church. They do not allow other people to give their testimonies or share what the Lord has done in their lives.

Sometimes when a person wants to be a witness for the Lord, the pastor of that church will go up to that person and waive a credential or degree in his or her face. The pastor will then say, "You can't do that. You don't have one of these."

I'm not talking to leaders or pastors who won't let someone preach because that person is not studying the Word. I am talking to leaders and pastors who don't let people speak in church just because they don't have any credentials or a certificate to hang on their wall. I am also talking about pastors who don't want to give anyone else permission to speak in their churches.

There is a terrible type of discrimination growing in the churches. It is a discrimination against anyone who did not go to a Bible college or training course. As soon as someone wants to get out of the church and do something for Jesus, certain pastors will waive their degrees and discourage theses desires.

What good is a certificate or a piece of paper? Can you learn all about God and how he works by going to a Bible college? Can any man learn about an infinite God in a finite amount of time?

Why then do we ask for credentials, degrees, and certificates when someone wants to be a witness for the Lord? There is no set procedure for reaching a soul for Christ. It is the Holy Spirit through all of us who reaches people for Him.

Do not discriminate against people who did not go to a Bible college, or do not have credentials or a degree, or have not memorized every verse of the Bible. Jesus called uneducated, ordinary men to be disciples. He did not call religious scholars.

I wish there would be Sundays where the pastor just asks people to come up and give a testimony of what Jesus has done for them during the week. The pulpit is meant for everyone to share and not just for an elected few with degrees and "ownership" of the church. We will all share His glory when we are in heaven.

Challenge

When you are envious of others, you are not concerned for their best interests. In fact you are plotting harm to the Lord's people.

Read Daniel chapter 6. As you read this, think to yourself if anyone ever tried to discourage you from doing something from the Lord because they thought that you weren't good enough or that you were a bad choice.

Have you ever discouraged another believer from doing what the Lord has called them to do?

Pray to the Lord to ask you for guidance concerning something the Lord put on your heart to do and see if the Lord wants you to do it. Ask the Lord also to show you anybody that you may have discouraged from following the Lord and ask the Lord for forgiveness.

If the Lord puts it on your heart to do something, you need to do it. Don't listen to pastors, friends, or family if you are certain that the Lord wants you to do it. Remember it is better to serve the Lord than man.

LESSON 27
Internet Prophets

"And he said, Take heed that ye be not deceived: for many shall come
in my name, saying, I am Christ, and the time draweth near: go ye not
therefore after them."
(Luke 21: 8)

This nation has done a lot of things that we as a nation need to repent of. Things such as the slave trade or the stealing of land from the native Americans, who were here before us.

People can have the best intentions and excuses for sin. However, any sin is wrong, even with the best intentions.

Woodstock was one of those events. About half a million people went there intending to stand in protest against the war and to find love. Instead it ended up being an event where other gods and people were worshipped. It became an event where people partook in lust and in drug abuse. Woodstock was almost declared a disaster.

The sins of our nation need to be repented of if America is going to stand. This next poem tells the story of what happened back in Woodstock back in 1969.

Poem/Song

Jesus Wept
Back in the summer of 1969.
There was a major shift in the paradigm.
In Vietnam, there was rumor of war.
This drove the U.S. into an uproar.
Americans asked why they should fight.
There was a desire for unity among black and white.
There was also talks about a woman's right.
For peace and unity America turned to fight.
So they planned a three day concert that would rock.
The name of this concert is called Woodstock.
People were searching for love and peace.

And for the war in Vietnam to cease.
In the town of Wallkill, it was planned for the need.
But due to protest, to a farm in Bethel it continued to proceed.
The reason for the gathering was good.
But people ended up not living like they should.
For instead of Jesus, they turned to other things.
Drugs, false god worship, and sexual sins as each band sings.
The tears from Heaven came down.
Because of all the sin that happened on the ground.
People continued to defy the rain.
And continued in their sin that was insane.
People became so misguided and confused.
From all the sin and being drug abused.
As those tears from Heaven continued to come down.
Each band continued with a different sound.
Woodstock was almost a disastrous event.
People were starving and ready to die in their tent.
But the Lord put compassion in other people's hearts.
To prepare food, provide shelter, and do their parts.
Today, as those tears from Heaven now and then come down.
We still have different protest groups around.
But why is it sometimes the Christians can't be found?
And instead bury their heads like ostriches in the ground.
Instead of hiding in our church country clubs,
We need to go out in the parks, malls, and pubs.
We need to stand for the Lord's peace and love.
Stand up to comfort the One who cries for us from above.
People are still searching for the truth.
We need to show them His Word like the book of Ruth.
We need to fight against worldly sin.
We need to scream and shout for Him.
For our freedom to worship Him, we must turn and fight.
Before we lose it all in just one night.
This is for the one whose tears come down.
Please comfort Him, repent, and turn your life around.

What Do You Think?

Beware of internet prophets. They claim that they predicted events such as 9/11.

I once saw an email from a so-called internet prophet that said Barrack Obama would never be inaugurated. Well, the day came, and Barrack Obama was inaugurated and became President of the United States. This prophecy was definitely false.

Jesus said that in the last days there will be false christs and false prophets. People will run here and there to see these people who claim to be sent from God or even that they are God.

Jesus warns us not to follow these people. They are ravenous wolves pretending to be sheep.

Look in the Bible and line up what people say with what the Bible says. When the Lord sends someone to prophesy, He will always provide some hope in His message. He always gives people a chance to repent and turn back to Him. Even when the Lord said that He would destroy a nation, He always sent someone to tell people to repent and provided hope for change if they did.

We should not be people who live on rumors and walk around in fear. The worst thing that can happen to us is that we die and go to heaven.

I can send emails out to everyone saying that I predicted 9/11. Don't believe everything displayed on the internet. Believe in what the Bible says.

We also should not spread gossip. This does not only apply to our lips but also through emails and text messages. It only brings fear, doubt, and discouragement.

Challenge

People, countries, and nations have done a lot of horrible things that have displeased the Lord.

Take some time right now to pray for the nation and different events that have happened in history that resulted in sin. Please pray that the nation will repent and turn back to the Lord.

Also ask the Lord to pray for repentance for not only yourself but for all your ancestors all the way back to Adam and Eve. Pray that the Lord will break any curses that have resulted from any sins and also pray that the Lord will heal your soul.

We need the Lord's grace and mercy. Without them, we do not have a chance to stand.

LESSON 28

Please Don't Send this Message to Ten People

"For we preach not ourselves, but Christ Jesus the Lord; and ourselves your servants for Jesus' sake." (2 Cori. 4: 5)

The Lord's love is meant to be shared. However, sometimes we struggle with telling others about Him. We are scared of being rejected. We are scared that we will be laughed at. The best way to resist this fear is by standing on His Word.

Remember how the disciples were beaten for their faith. They considered it an honor when they suffered for the Lord. Remember greater is He that is in you than he that is in the world.

This next poem has two speakers. Speaker 1 is someone reading from Mark chapter sixteen verses fifteen to twenty. Speaker 2 represents the fear and worry we struggle with when we preach the Word. See how scripture can help you in times of fear and doubt as you preach the Gospel to others.

Poem/Song

Go Ye Into All the World

Speaker 1

> And Jesus said unto them, "Go Ye into all the world and preach the Gospel to every creature." (Mark 16:15)

Speaker 2

> Whoa Whoa Whoa!!!!
> Hi my name is Mr. WhatIf.
> Sorry to interrupt your spiritual lift.
> But are you nuts talking to that boy or girl!!
> There are a lot of dangers out there in the world.
> What if they think that you're no fun?
> What if they are carrying a knife or gun?

What if they won't let you turn and run?
And Bang, you're done.

Speaker 1

"No Weapon that is formed against me will prosper" (Isai. 54:17)

Speaker 2

Yea, but what if they think you're an imposter.
I mean, face it you ain't no saint.
What if you can't speak and instead faint.
You will be chopped, cooked, and diced.

Speaker 1

"And if children, the heirs, heirs of God, joint heirs of Christ.
If so be that we suffer with Him, that we may be also glorified together."
(Roma. 8:17)

Speaker 2

Whoa Whoa Whoa!! What you say out there will be remembered forever.
What if you say something that will make them sad?
What if you say something that will make them mad?
And they decide to do something to you that's bad?
What if you dishonor your mom and dad?
What about the possible emotional pain?

Speaker 1:

"To live is Christ, to die is gain." (Phil. 1:21)
You know, Mr. Whatif, there's one thing you'll never claim.
What if that person becomes saved in Jesus' name!!!!!!!!
"And they went forth and preached everywhere. The Lord working with
them with signs following. Amen!!" (Mark 16:20)

What Do You Think?

If you are not ashamed of Jesus, send this message to ten people right now.
Send this message to ten people right now and God will give you a special
blessing twenty-four hours from now.
I don't care what you are doing. I'm ordering you to drop what you are
doing and send this to ten people right now. Don't delete this message or
you will burn in hell.

I'll bet almost everyone reading this book has gotten a message with something at the end of it like one of the three messages just mentioned. When you receive an email with one of these messages, you're ordered to stop what you are doing, think of ten people to send the email to, and send the same message to them, including the person who sent it to you. If you delete the email instead of sending it to ten people, you feel like you let God down.

I'm not saying you should stop sending emails which lead people to Christ. I am just saying that when you send an email about Christ, please don't put one of these messages at the end of it.

Some of you may be saying, "Where is your Faith?" or, "If you are a true follower of Jesus Christ, you wouldn't mind sending these emails to ten people." I have to be honest. I usually delete them instead of sending them to anyone. Sometimes I am too busy to send them. Other times I feel ashamed to send emails with such messages attached at the end to my friends.

I would have to ask you, "Where is your faith?" Most of us reading this book should be older than children in kindergarten. We should send emails because we love Jesus and not because someone orders us to. If an email contains a message that truly comes from the Lord, I believe it will touch people so powerfully that they will just naturally resend the messages to other people. We still have the Bible today, despite all the attempts people have made to extinguish it. The Lord has protected his Word and the Bible is still one of the most read books in the world today. Do you think the Lord will lose an email just because it does not have one of these messages attached to the end of it?

When you send an email in the future, please delete such messages before you send it to those ten people. I would like to get an email about the Lord which resembles this:

Jesus Loves You
You do not have to do anything with this message.
It is okay to delete it.
Jesus loves you whether you send this message or not.
You will not be any more blessed if you send this email.
You are blessed because Jesus loves you.
Accept Him into your heart, soul and life.
Just give Him a chance and He will show you all the blessings He has for you.

Challenge

For those of you who still want to prove their faith, I got an assignment for you. No simple click of the mouse this time.

1. Turn off or log off of your computer.
2. Get up out of that comfortable computer chair.
3. Leave your comfy computer room, workstation, or cubicle.
4. Find a neighbor, coworker, or someone who is not on your email list.
5. Invite that person out to lunch or to your house for dinner.
6. Get to know them, and if the opportunity arises, share the Word with them. Maybe you can add another email address to your list.

The Lord did not say simply to mail letters and send emails all over the world. Jesus said, "Go ye into all the world and preach the Gospel.

LESSON 29

Success When You Fail

"Choosing rather to suffer affliction with the people of God, than to enjoy the pleasures of sin for a season; Esteeming the reproach of Christ greater riches than the treasures in Egypt: for he had respect unto the recompence of the reward." (Hebr. 11: 25-26)

Sometimes when we are serving the Lord, we don't see what the Lord is doing right away. Sometimes it is like we are struggling and struggling and nothing is getting done. Rejoice in the Lord and know that He is still working in your situation. Keep on serving Him and focus on Him.

This next poem is about the story of Moses. Moses had to go to the Pharaoh many times before Pharaoh finally let the Israelites go. Moses left everything to follow the Lord and help His people. Not only that, His own people turned on Him so many times. In addition, Pharaoh could of had Moses killed at any time when he approached him. Yet, even in these situations Moses still obeyed the Lord. To live is Christ. To die is gain.

Poem/Song

The Stubborn Pharaoh
Here is a story most of you know.
About a Pharaoh who was stubborn and slow.
He had such a hatred for the Jews.
He ordered them to be enslaved and abused.
One day a man named Moses popped up.
This was when all Hell would erupt.
The water in the Nile, Moses turned to blood.
This attempt to impress Pharaoh was a dud.
The Egyptians started to complain and moan.
They sang this song with a groan.

Chorus

Oh Pharaoh, Pharaoh
We want to know?
When you gonna let those people go?
Oh Pharaoh, Pharaoh
Are you so slow?
There's a bigger God who's the star of the show.
Oh Pharaoh, Pharaoh
Just let them go.
Or else we'll end up like the dodo.
Oh Pharaoh, Pharaoh
We want to know?
When you gonna let those people go?
When you gonna let those people go?
After the blood, Pharaoh hardened his heart.
To let them go, Pharaoh wouldn't hear a part.
So Moses called on his God to bring frogs.
They came up out of the ponds and bogs.
They were loose in the houses and street.
Pharaoh then said he would change his beat.
Pharaoh said he would let them go.
Moses prayed and the frogs left with one blow.
Pharaoh then changed his mind.
This caused a lot of trouble to unwind.
The Egyptians started to complain and moan.
They sang this song with a groan.

Chorus

The God of Moses sent more plagues and disease.
But Pharaoh continued still unappeased.
The God of Moses sent lice and flies.
But once these plaques were gone, Pharaoh still lies.
Our farm animals are sick and dying.
Each plague get worse with the Pharaoh's lying.
These plagues gave the Egyptians more toils.
Especially when they were getting boils.
The Egyptians begged to let the people go.
After all this, Pharaoh still told them no.
The Egyptians started to complain and moan.
They sang this song with a groan.

Chorus

Because those previous plagues didn't light a spark.
Even in the daytime, Egypt was in the dark.
The same routine happened time after time.
When the plagues were lifted, Pharaoh changed his mind.
The God of Moses caused it to hail.
This made the Egyptians cry and wail.
Pharaoh's heart was still hard as stone.
He would first agree than change his tone.
The next plague was of locusts.
Pharaoh still just wouldn't focus.
The Egyptians started to complain and moan.
They sang this song with a groan.

Chorus

After all these plagues, there came one more.
An angel killed the first person any woman bore.
There was death and wailing all over the land.
Pharaoh ordered them to go with one command.
So the people are gone, the plagues were over.
But Pharaoh started to feel like a pushover.
He sent his army to get them at the Red Sea.
This was a mistake, Pharaoh should have let them be.
All his men got killed and drowned.
The Egyptians did nothing but frowned.
The Egyptians started to complain and moan.
They sang this song with a groan.

Chorus

What Do You Think?

Things in this life are uncertain. Sometimes we will succeed in what we do and sometimes we will fail. Sometimes the Lord will tell us to do things in which there is no chance of success in our own eyes.

Don't let fear of failure run your life. Sometimes we are afraid to share about Jesus because we think we will say and do the wrong thing and lead our family and friends to a worse place than before.

Sometimes we think of ourselves as hypocrites because we tell others to worship and serve the Lord yet we still fall back into sin. Do not let fear of failure keep you from doing His work.

In the Bible, people acted by faith. They did not know what God would do. Big companies like Dell and A T & T were formed by people who didn't know if their companies would succeed or fail.

This book may fail. People may take this book and throw it in the fire. It may be banned from churches and forbidden to be read.

I must write because the Lord told me to write this book. Friends may hate me. The press may speak badly about me. The government may hunt me down and imprison me. However, I still must write this book to share what the Lord has shown me in my life.

There are two types of failure. The first failure is not doing anything to better yourself because you have given up. This is an awful type of failure because you always wonder if you would have had a chance had you tried.

The second type of "failure" involves trying even though things don't go as you hoped. In this case, you feel certain that something went wrong.

I would rather have things go wrong and be in the Lord's will than "succeed" and be out of His will. In the end, we will all have to give an account to Him for our lives.

Challenge

Remember, when you are in the Lord's will, you never really fail. You may feel like you have failed, because human understanding cannot always grasp God's purpose, and His future plans. He works everything together for our good.

Read Exodus chapters 7 to 14. As you read this ask yourself if you have any stubbornness that needs to be repented off. Is there an area of your life that you are keeping from God because you want to control that area?

Ask the Lord to remove any stubbornness from you. Also ask the Lord to give you strength and obedience to do what the Lord says no matter what the result. Ask the Lord to remove any fear of speaking about the Lord and to give you love for His people.

Are we going to live with fear of failure in our hearts, or are we determined to keep going above all else?

Though it may look like we've failed, we will achieve victory.

Whatsoever thy hand findeth to do, do it with thy might;

for there is no work, nor device, nor knowledge, nor wisdom, in the grave whither thou goest.

I returned, and saw under the sun, that the race is not to the swift,

nor the battle to the strong, neither yet bread to the wise, nor yet riches to men of understanding, nor yet favour to men of skill; but time and chance happeneth to them all.

For man also knoweth not his time:

as the fishes that are taken in an evil net, and as the birds that are caught in the snare; so are the sons of men snared in an evil time, when it falleth suddenly upon them.

(Eccl. 9: 10-12)

LESSON 30
Keep your Eyes on the Prize

"Hear me when I call, O God of my righteousness: thou hast enlarged me
when I was in distress; have mercy upon me, and hear my prayer."
(Psal. 4:1)

It can be tough to keep your eyes focused on Jesus with so much going on in this world. With all the distractions and problems associated with this fallen world, it can be hard to see a Lord who is good, loving, and faithful.

We have to keep reminding ourselves sometimes that our eternal rewards are not down here. They are in Heaven. The greatest reward anyone can hope for is for eternity with our Lord and Savior Jesus Christ. I wonder sometimes if heaven would be heaven without God.

This next life experience is about how I had to trust the Lord for a position in accounting. Job hunting is hard work. It can be very easy to give up the search and do nothing.

Life Experience

While going for my MBA degree, I worked at a couple of different jobs. In the spring of 2003, I worked as a tax preparer for H & R Block.

I took the position so that I could get some office experience. The job was all right. It helped me pay off the car loan I had on my 2002 Toyota Camry. I also took the tax course that the company offered.

Their tax course was a lot better than the one I took in college. I would advise anyone who files tax returns to take the H & R Block tax course.

However, I did not like working with the company's computer program, called TPS (Tax Preparation Software). It was a long, drawn out process just to do someone's tax return. If there was a question, you had to go through the whole process before you could go back to answer the question. The owner of the franchise was not the friendliest person to work with either.

After the tax season was over, I wanted something more permanent instead of just seasonal. I still worked for Kmart while working for H & R Block.

After the job with H & R Block was over, I continued going to interviews and job fairs with no success until May 2004. In May, I decided to get out of Kmart and work somewhere else, because people in human resources still saw me as a customer service associate instead of as an accountant. I got a job with RGIS. RGIS is a company that helps audit the inventory for various stores. I helped them do an audit of a Price Chopper that used to be in Poughkeepsie, NY.

About two days after I accepted this job, I got an offer to work for Accountemps in White Plains, New York. Accountemps is a temp agency that offers jobs with various companies. I also got an offer to work for the post office in Kingston, New York as a mail clerk.

It is interesting. For years, you don't find anything, and all of a sudden everyone wants to hire you at the same time. I prayed to the Lord and I decided to take the job with Accountemps.

Accountemps offered temporary positions with other companies that may become permanent. They got me a job as a junior accountant with Fuji film in Valhalla, New York. The job was supposed to last till the end of the summer. I quit RGIS, gave my two weeks notice at Kmart, and prepared to work for Fuji.

After the second day on the job, Accountemps notified me that the job was over. I don't know why Fuji let me go. I think it was because they had an audit team come into the department I was working in to cut jobs. I prayed to the Lord for guidance, since I'd turned down the other two jobs and given notice at Kmart. I continued to believe in the Lord for a job and I still planned on leaving Kmart.

About a week later, I received another call from Accountemps about an accounting clerk position in Hawthorne, New York, at a marketing firm called The Listworks Corporation. They said the job was only supposed to last a week.

I accepted the job since I had nothing else planned. One week turned into two, and weeks turned into months. I worked in the billing department, doing the billing, recording incoming checks, and applying payments to the invoices that were paid. They offered me a position in their accounts receivable department permanently, but the Lord warned me not to take it because it was not going to last.

I worked as a temp for The Listworks Corporation for seven months. The job would have lasted longer, but the company was forced to declare bankruptcy and went out of business.

The Listworks Corporation had a great family atmosphere. Even though the company went out of business, a lot of the people who worked there still meet once a month at the Westchester Diner near Peekskill, New York, and continue to keep in touch.

What Do You Think?

Keep your eyes on the prize. Do not settle for riches in this life.

These riches will pass away. Keep your eyes on Jesus, who offers the greatest gift of all. Jesus has allowed us to go to a better place.

Why do we cry for people at funerals? I wonder if they are up in heaven crying for us because we still have to live in this present world.

I wonder also if there are people in hell who are crying for loved ones who are still living on the earth and who don't know Jesus. At least when my parents die, I know that they will be in heaven.

It is hard not to cry over a loved one when you don't know if their soul will go to heaven or hell. We can only trust that they are in the Lord's hands. This is the safest place to be. We need to prepare for when we die or when He comes back, whichever is sooner.

Challenge

"Behold, he cometh with clouds; and every eye shall see him, and they also which pierced him: and all kindreds of the earth shall wail because of him. Even so, Amen." (Reve. 1:7)

Pray to the Lord to help you not to forget about treasures in heaven and to forget about treasures on earth. Ask the Lord to help you keep your eyes on Him through the good times as well as the bad. Keep your eyes on Jesus, who is the ultimate prize.

LESSON 31
The Pharmaceutical Company

"These things I have spoken unto you, that in me ye might have peace. In the world ye shall have tribulation: but be of good cheer; I have overcome the world." (John 16:33)

The Lord is calling us to be soldiers for Him. We need to live for Him and trust Him with our lives. We need to show the world who we serve.

Sometimes, we do not speak up for the Word of the Lord because we fear people. We need to continue to walk blameless and share His light.

This next poem is about being an example for Jesus Christ. As we live for Jesus, people will see the light of Christ through us.

Poem/Song

Let Your Light Shine Before Men
Whether it is day or night
Remember that Jesus is the Light.
Let the Light in you illuminate.
Share with everyone. Don't discriminate.
Let Jesus through you show His might.
So that your glow can be out of sight.
Remember, don't do wrong but do right.
So that your glow will remain bright.
In this world that is so dark.
We are called to light a spark.
Don't walk around scared and uptight.
I hope to encourage you as I write.
Let the Light fly free like a kite.
Give Him the reigns and let Him take flight.
Shine in the nighttime as the moon.
Shine as the sun in the afternoon.
Shine the Light from the valleys and heights.

Put on the armor of God as valiant knights.
Shine bright as floodlights.
Burn bright as candle lights.
Don't hide the Light under pails.
Proclaim the Light, so darkness fails.
Stop the Devil's bug bites.
And shine bright as flashlights.
Get up and fight.
The world's dark fright.
Let the Light shine as a flame.
Proclaim in Jesus name.
Be pure and cleansed white.
With the Light, darkness we will smite.

Life Experience

The Listworks Corporation was a great place to work. It was a family work environment since it was such a small office.

The great thing about this job was that it gave me accounting experience. It is hard to get that first bit of experience when looking for a job.

After the Listworks Corporation went bankrupt and closed down, I went back to looking for another job. It was about two months before I got another temp job for a different temp agency called Advantage. I ended up working at a pharmaceutical company called Boehringer Ingelheim in Ridgefield, Connecticut.

This was a big company. It occupied a lot of land, with many different buildings. There were hiking paths where people could walk during breaks. This company also had a great cafeteria. There were always many options to choose from for lunch.

I worked in the accounts payable department. Another temp and I were the only men in the department. We were also the two youngest.

I was covering a woman who had been transferred to another department to work on a project. I was in charge of paying the creditors that began with the letters C and Q.

When I first started, the company was changing computer programs. They were switching from SAP 4.5 to SAP 4.7.

This job helped me in several ways. I had to answer the phones. Before this job, I had a terrible fear of talking on the phone. Sometimes the Lord puts us in positions to help us overcome our fears.

It also helped me learn to work around women. I had a couple of guy friends, but I'd never had any friends who were women. It wasn't that I was a chauvinist. I was just really shy. Sometimes, this nice woman in my department would invite me to go to lunch with her. Gradually, I overcame some of my shyness working and being around women.

Besides the people in my department, I did not make too many friends working there. I did meet one guy who would drive all the important people of the company to the airport and other places. He would tell me stories about how his son traveled cross country and how he said it was the best thing he ever did.

The Lord puts us in places for a time and season so that He can do a work in us. When I left that job seven months later, I had all my bills paid. The woman that I was covering completed her project, and I was back to looking for a job.

Challenge

The Lord is calling us to be a light. However, in order to become a light for Christ we must put away the fear and darkness out of our lives.

Some of you may be going through a trial that is forcing you to face your fears. Pray to the Lord for deliverance from any fear that you may have. Pray against any fear of people, fear of failure, and fear of rejection especially.

LESSON 32
G. E.

"Now therefore arise, O Lord God, into thy resting place, thou, and the
ark of thy strength: let thy priests O Lord God, be clothed with salvation,
and let thy saints rejoice in goodness." (2 Chron. 6: 41)

The Bible says that the world will hate us because the world hates Jesus. If we are truly walking in the Lord, the world will hate us since we are not following the norm. People are going to call us strange and weird. We cannot let this fear of what people think control our lives. We need to focus on what the Lord says.

This next poem is a story about Noah and the ark. Before Noah sailed on the ark it never rained. Water falling from the sky was unheard of.

Poem/Song

Insane About the Rain
A long time ago before there was rain
There was a man named Noah, who people called insane.
Before the rain, there was a watery mist all over the land
That kept everything cool and prevented it from getting tanned.
The Lord told Noah that he would flood the Earth.
Because man did what was evil from the moment of their birth.
He said that He would send this water from the sky.
And everything on the Earth was going to die.
The Lord told Noah to build an ark.
Among Noah's neighbors, a song started to spark.
**They call him
Cuckoo.
They call him
Loo Loo.
Noah has just gone nutty and insane.
They called him
Cuckoo.
They called him
Loo Loo.
Noah can't stop talkin about this rain.**

Here's a word from me to you.
He's Cuckoo.
The ark was to be three hundred by fifty by thirty cubits high.
Noah was obedient to the Lord with his reply.
He built the ark so he wouldn't die.
He worked on the ark every day.
Even when the people came to sing and say.
They call him.
Cuckoo
They call him
Loo Loo.
If you want a crackpot, you just hit the jackpot.
They call him.
Cuckoo
They call him
Loo Loo.
If you want someone nutty, you just found a buddy.
Here's a word from me to you.
He's Cuckoo.
The people told Noah that He was way out there.
Noah focused on the Lord, he did not care.
The Lord told him to get animals in pairs,
the lions, the tigers, and the bears.
He loaded up all the mammals and birds.
He did not care about people's sung words.
They call him.
Cuckoo
They call him
Loo Loo.
Noah's bananas. his mind is hazy
They call him.
Cuckoo
They call him
Loo Loo.
Noah's bonkers, He's just gone crazy.
Here's a word from me to you.
He's Cuckoo.
Noah continued to collect deer and moose.
The people replied, "Noah has a screw loose."
Noah collected the sheep and the goats.
The people were shouting for the men in white coats.
As he loaded up the rabbits, turtles, and hares,
People sang and replied with their stares.
They call him.
Cuckoo

They call him
Loo Loo.
"Noah's has bats, there in his belfry
They call him.
Cuckoo
They call him
Loo Loo.
Noah's got rats, that can't be healthy.
Here's a word from me to you.
He's Cuckoo.
Noah collected the salamanders and frogs
And loaded them on the ark made of logs.
He gathered up his sons, his daughters-in-law, and wife.
He loaded them into the ark to save their life.
What people said, Noah didn't care a thing.
The mob of people continued to sing.
They call him.
Cuckoo
They call him
Loo Loo.
Noah says we should repent of our sin.
They call him.
Cuckoo
They call him
Loo Loo.
Someone please call for him the loony bin.
Here's a word from me to you.
He's Cuckoo.
The people continued to joke and clown.
But then, there was heard this thundering sound.
BOOM
What is this that is now coming down.
It is water hitting the ground.
The people started to scream and shout.
Knowing that Noah wasn't so way out.
It rained for forty days and forty nights.
The water covered all the mountainous heights.
Noah was by now very glad.
That He listened to the Lord and was not bad.
When people say you are a Jesus freak.
Consider it strength and not as weak.
When you follow the Lord, people will say you're strange.
Don't listen to them, and in the Lord's task engage.
When people in this world call you nuts.
Remember Noah's story whenever the rain erupts.

Life Experience

I didn't have to wait long. I got another job working as a temp at General Electric (GE) in Danbury, Connecticut. I worked in the personal property tax department. I had to pay all of the personal property tax bills.

The employees at G. E. were very friendly people. However, they were also a bunch of wiseguys. They would do things like beep your horn while you were driving and trick you into crazy bets like drinking a gallon of milk in under two hours without throwing up.

It was definitely a fun environment. The job was very easy to do. I also rarely had to call people. I just worked on a big pile of tax bills which was usually over a foot high.

The big thing I learned at this job was not to take life too seriously. People will intentionally and unintentionally say negative things about you and joke around with you, but it doesn't mean you have to roll over and cry. Petty arguments are not worth loosing friends over and holding grudges. Just worry about what the Lord says about your life and go by that.

I also learned that you can be the best worker for the job but if the Lord has not called you to that position, you will not get it. I was one of the best workers in the department.

A year later, they let me go because if they had renewed my contract, they would have had to pay me for health benefits.

On the last day of this job, I got an interview at a company that does the accounting for bread distributors. I went to interview and I got the job. After all the years of praying, the Lord answered my prayers about finding a permanent job in accounting.

Challenge

Have you ever been offended by anyone for serving the Lord? Did you ever reveal to someone something that the Lord showed you and they just criticized you or laughed in your face.

Sometimes the things we are called to do for the Lord will sound strange to other people. Remember, the Lord uses the foolish things to confound the wise.

Read Genesis chapters 6 and 7. As you read, ask the Lord for healing from any wounds that may have formed from people calling you names or for criticizing your ministry. Ask the Lord to forgive them.

LESSON 33
The Job Market

"Recompense to no man evil for evil. Provide things honest in the sight of
all men." (Roma. 12: 17)

The Lord desires to spend time with us. However, sometimes we are so busy doing things that we end up hardly spending any time with Him.

Sometimes we do all these things that we think are good for the Lord when the Lord has not called us to do those things.

This next poem is about taking the time to be quiet and letting the Lord show you what things you are suppose to do. When you see the word "knock" in bold you are suppose to be knocking on something.

Poem/Song

The Knocking
Let's see. Today is Sunday.
We have church today.
We have to show up early for seating.
(sound of knocking) Knock, Knock, Knock
Tomorrow night we have a prayer meeting.
(sound of knocking) Knock, Knock, Knock
Tuesday, I sing in the choir.
Wednesday night is the church bonfire.
(sound of knocking) Knock, Knock, Knock
Thursday night is the church Little League game.
Friday night, I'm busy doing the same.
(sound of knocking) Knock, Knock, Knock
Saturday morning, I volunteer downtown at the food drive.
In the afternoon, I do the yard work and spray another beehive.
(sound of knocking) Knock, Knock, Knock
At night, we have company for dinner in the den.
The following week it is the same thing again.
(sound of knocking) Knock, Knock, Knock

I don't know, I thought we were suppose to feel free.
But look at my schedule, how can this be.
(sound of knocking) Knock, Knock, Knock
I thought His yoke was suppose to be light.
But I feel like I'm working all day and night.
(sound of knocking) Knock, Knock, Knock
I work, care for my loved ones, and do these things that are good.
but I feel that I don't hear from Him like I should.
(sound of knocking) Knock, Knock, Knock
Is it possible that I am not doing enough?
And I just make excuses with all of this stuff?
Is it possible that I am doing too much?
That I don't take the time to feel His touch?
(sound of knocking) Knock, Knock, Knock
I need to take a good look.
Through my appointment book.
(sound of knocking) Knock, Knock, Knock
Lord please show me what ministries you want me to do.
I want to serve, but I also want to hear from you.
Those things not of you, please help remove.
New things you want me to do, help me get into the groove.
(sound of knocking) Knock, Knock, Knock
Who is there? Oh the Lord, it is Him.
I need to open up the door and let Him in.

What Do You Think

Opportunity knocks all the time. There are so many chances to proclaim the Lord to other people in our lives.

It is funny how we can think of things to do when we are too busy to do them. However, when we have the time to do them, we forget all about them.

The Lord helps me get through each and every day. Some days can be very long. Some days can be very rainy and gloomy.

How things change in the twinkling of an eye! The job market and job interviews can be very tough sometimes. Interviews can be so subjective. There is also a lot of favoritism in the workplace. You can be fully qualified for a position, but; people will deny you simply because they don't like you.

Take heart, because the Lord has the final say and He chooses the people He wants in each and every position. He has a position for me and He certainly has a position for you.

Challenge

Is the Lord trying to speak to you but things are too busy? Do you set aside a part of your day just to seek Him for direction?

Look through your weekly schedule and look at all your plans for that week. Ask the Lord how He wants you to spend your time. Ask Him what things He wants you to do and what things He does not want you to do. Make sure you constantly spend some time in His presence.`

LESSON 34
True Worship

"Whom having not seen, ye love; in whom, though now ye see him not,
yet believing, ye rejoice with joy unspeakable and full of glory:" (I Pet. 1:8)

Worship is on the verge of dying out in our churches. At church, we don't raise our hands and dance like we should. We are too concerned with what people think. I was in one church where they told my family that lifting our hands was distracting and our worship discouraged new believers from coming.

This is a lie from the enemy. The Bible says that the joy of the Lord is our strength.

This next poem addresses the issue of worshipping the Lord freely in the Lord's house. How can we find joy in the Lord if our worshipping Him is hindered? As our forefathers came to this nation to worship the Lord freely, so must we.

Poem/Song

Distraction
Is there something wrong with me?
But how in the churches can this be?
I want to worship and praise God and His Son.
I guess I was having too much fun.
When did worshipping freely become a sin;?
This is why in church I don't fit in.
When they start the music and praise
And my arms and hands I start to raise.
That some people come right up to you
And tell you your dancing you just can't do.
The Devil will send in these deceivers
to say that the dancing discourages new believers.
When you want to worship with your action
They will tell you that your worship is a distraction.
I don't mean to cause any attention,
but I don't want to be put in detention.

I don't want to move my body to the groove
Just to be told to go in the back room.
How does the Holy Spirit in the church have a chance
When we cannot sing, worship freely, and dance?
Praise is a weapon against any demon
When you praise the Lord freely, they start screamin.
Satan and his demons want to stop you worshipping at any cost.
When people criticize your worship, count it a blessing and not a loss.
The Devil doesn't want you to scream and shout.
He will try to get you to cut it out.
Must I serve man more than the Lord?
Must I stand there expressionless as a board?
How other people worship, should I criticize?
Just to fit neatly in a church enterprise.
Doesn't the Lord love it when his people sing praise.
Instead of them standing there in a daze.
Should I judge people worshipping so true.
Instead of keeping my eyes focused on You.
Remember, in the Bible when David danced,
Michal saw how he worshipped and pranced
She laughed at him and started to joke;
Her dreams for children went up in smoke.
Beware, when you see someone around,
and for worshipping freely you put them down.
The church is supposed to encourage people to sing and shout,
Not to discourage worship by casting them out.
It's like chopping off your arm if it is in pain;
To tell people not to worship in church is insane.
Worshipping and dancing for the Lord is not a sin.
Maybe that is why Jesus Christ doesn't fit in.
Just concentrate on how you worship the Lord.
Worship freely the One who should be adored.
Remember that you are doing it for Him.
Remember that worshipping the Lord is not a sin.
Just like them, you have the right.
To worship Him any way in His sight.
You are not there to please others in the church.
You are not there just to sit on a perch.
You should feel free to scream, dance, and shout.
Continue to worship freely even when a church kicks you out.

What Do You Think?

Worship is one of the most important actions that a believer in Christ can do.

Reading the Bible is very important. However, some people just read it like any other book or newspaper. They only read it just to look religious.

Memorizing scripture is important. However, some people just memorize it for an exam in Bible class or to make themselves look more religious.

Prayer is very important also, but some people use it as only a 911 call when they are in trouble. Other people just pray to look religious. Prayer is meant to be communication with the Lord. We are supposed to talk to the Lord just like we talk to a friend or family member. Prayer is also supposed to work both ways. We are supposed to listen to the Lord just like we listen to our friends and family members when they speak.

Tithing is very important. The question is, are you doing it because you love the Lord or are you doing it just to get God off your back and look religious doing it?

Helping others and working in ministries is also great, but are you doing it for the Lord's glory or for your own self-esteem?

True worship, I believe, is the only thing a believer does that is done solely for the Lord. Our worship shows the Lord how we really reverence Him. It also shows the Lord we understand that He is a mighty, awesome, and good God.

Do we just stand there like stiffs and mouth the words without thinking? Do we dance and embrace the Holy Spirit when He comes in the midst of the worship? Why is it that when we are at a club, we dance to the music, yet when we have worship, we just stand there.

When we get to heaven, are you just going to stand there? I don't think so.

You will probably be jumping up and down singing and dancing before the Lord.

Do we just show up when the pastor is preaching and skip the worship altogether. If we had an invitation to meet a president or a wealthy individual, we would be sure to be on time if we were personally invited. How much more can the Holy Spirit provide? Yet, we don't even bother showing up when God is giving authority and power to His people.

Worship is fellowship time with the Lord. We always go out of our way to hang out with our friends and family. Why should the Lord be any different? Set that alarm clock, get up for the worship, and spend time with the Lord.

Do we just look at other people while the worship is going on and try to figure out who is really worshiping and who is just a hypocrite? Why are you judging others to see if their worship is serious or if they are being hypocritical?

If you are looking at people during the worship and making remarks about them, you are not worshipping the Lord. Worship the Lord and spend time with Him. Let the Lord decide who is serious and who is being hypocritical.

Challenge

Read 2 Samuel 6: 12-23. In the Bible, David danced many times before the Lord. Sometimes he danced in a linen ephod. This is like dancing in your underwear. David was not composed and standing still before the Lord. He went bananas before the Lord.

Once you finish reading, just play some music and get into worshipping Him. Even if the music is outdated and off key, just fellowship with the Lord and spend time with Him.

Don't be afraid to show the Lord who you really are in Him. Take some time to just worship and praise the Lord.

But love ye your enemies, and do good, and lend, hoping for nothing again;

and your reward shall be great, and ye shall be the children of the Highest: for He is kind unto the unthankful and to the evil.

Be ye therefore merciful,

as your Father also is merciful.

Judge not, and ye shall not be judged:

condemn not, and ye shall not be condemned: forgive, and ye shall be forgiven:

Give, and it shall be given unto you;

good measure, pressed down, and shaken together, and running over, shall men give into your bosom. For with the same measure that ye mete withal it shall be measured to you again.

(Luke 6: 35-38)

LESSON 35

Permanent Job at Last

"For thou, Lord, art good, and ready to forgive; and plenteous in mercy
unto all them that call upon thee." (Psal. 86: 5)

As people, we sometimes try to come up with a formula for God. We try to figure out God so that we can do the least work possible to serve Him.

This next poem will show how the Lord is looking for people that will go all the way for Him. Not just a part of the way or half way. The Lord wants people that will surrender their whole life to Him.

Poem/Song

How Much?
How long should I pray?
I have other things to do today.
How long should I read His Word?
A chapter, a verse, nobody has concurred.
At least I know tithing is ten percent,
Just enough to make a sizeable dent.
A thought has occurred I have to claim:
What if the Lord also thought the same?
What if God said "That is enough for today."
And went back up to heaven and left me to stay.
What if he quit after my first sin?
Imagine the agony we all would be in.
What if He left me when I was born.
I think my fate would be as the unicorn.
What if He said "enough" back in the past?
Our whole future would end so fast.
What if He said "Enough of this stuff!"
When Hitler was in charge?
The pilgrims voyaged on their barge.
What if He left in 1492,

129

When Columbus sailed the ocean blue.
What if He left in the middle ages?
Our history books would be blank pages.
What if He said "Enough!" after He died on the cross?
Without His Spirit to guide us, we would all be lost.
What if He said "Enough!" after Adam and Eve ate the fruit?
All humanity would be lost when He gave them the boot.
I'm not saying to pray all night and day.
I'm not saying to fast every day.
So that you become anorexic,
To the point where you need a paramedic.
It is not about quantity but about quality.
Love Him enough to show Him your honesty,
Just enough to show the Lord gratitude.
Let His love flow through your attitude.

Life Experience

I was so glad when I finally got a permanent job. I had health benefits and paid vacations, which the temp jobs never provided.

This was a small, friendly office. However, I had to do a lot of work to get to where I am today.

There was a coworker who left the company shortly after I was hired. He said that he needed some time to study for the CPA exam. When he left, it was found that he was months behind in processing his monthly profit and loss statements. Everyone was calling and complaining about not having them.

It was later discovered that he actually left so that he could set up his own company and compete against us. I can't prove it, but I believe he deliberately sabotaged his accounts.

It was the end of the 2006 tax year. Everything was due, quarterly payroll forms, sales tax returns, 1120-S forms, and 1040 forms.

I got a ton of calls every day. There were so many days I felt like banging my head on the desk. I had to work Saturdays and Sundays to fix the accounts and keep up with everything. I also had to learn everything on my own, which was another hurdle to overcome.

It took a lot of organization, prayer, and time to get me through that tax season. A couple of clients left the company but many clients from back then we still have today.

Once tax season was over, the job was a lot easier. I also made a lot of improvements to how things were done.

Now, my job is such a blessing and I get to help people with their reports and tax questions. I still have days when I leave feeling bad, but I know the Lord will help me through it, one day at a time.

Life is unfair, but the Holy Spirit will give you the determination to not give up. I had to keep forgiving that coworker so many times for what he did. Forgiveness is an ongoing process and not just a one- time thing.

Challenge

A lot of people think that Salvation is just a once-in-a-lifetime confession in which you tell the Lord you are a sinner, ask Jesus into your life, and then go on with your life like nothing ever happened. Salvation is an ongoing thing. You should constantly ask the Lord to come into your life and repent of your sins every day.

Don't ever get to a point where you don't think you need any more Jesus or that "God time" is over. Being content with a little bit of Jesus just isn't enough.

Take this time to repeat the prayer in the back of this book. As you pray, ask the Lord to give you more love to serve Him and His people no matter what they have done to you.

LESSON 36

How to Get Revenge on the Devil

"Be not overcome of evil, but overcome evil with good." (Roma. 12: 21)

God loves us more than any of us could even imagine. How He could love a sinner like me is unbelievable. Thank you, Lord, that You are slow to anger, or none of us would still be alive.

This next poem was written to help express the love of the Lord. Even with our shortcomings, the Lord is always looking to bless us more.

Poem/Song

God's Heart
In the beginning, God existed right from the start.
God the Father, God the Son, and the Holy Spirit are all one part.
God is the very definition of love.
So God looked down from up above.
Love cannot be kept, it must be shared.
So God created the world to show He cared.
God's love continued to go long.
God's heart beat with this song.

Chorus

More More More More.
I have so much more in store.
More More More More.
My love reaches to the core.
More More More More.
I just want to love and adore.
More More More More.
I just wanna give so much More.
So God created the light and the air
Knowing what God the Son would one day bear.
God created the land and the seas;
These gifts could not set His heart at ease,

So he created the stars, moon, and sun on day four.
The Lord desired to love more.
God's love is perfect. It can't go wrong.
God's heart beat with this song.

Chorus

The Lord had more for us in store.
He created the fish in the sea and the birds on the shore.
The Lord lovingly created every animal and plant.
From the largest whale to the smallest ant.
The Lord lovingly created His biggest fan.
The Lord, in His own image, created man.
One more thing to finish off the creation of the world;
So that the man would not be lonely, He created a girl.
His love today continues to prolong.
God's heart beats with this song.

Chorus:

God walked with the man and the woman every day.
He desired to hear what they had to say.
He created a garden where they could live.
There was so much more He wanted to give.
He only had one decree:
To not eat fruit from just one tree.
Sadly this decree was broken and in came sin.
This multiplied greatly to separate us from Him.
So, out of love, the Lord sent His Son to die
So that we can be with Him who reigns on high.
Even with our faults, His love continues to stay strong.
God's heart beats with this song.

Chorus

God has a plan for you and me.
He loves you more than you will ever see.
Even at times when we question and doubt
He still remains faithful and helps us out.
It is His prayer that we desire Him more
So that we can find out what He has in store.
He has plans to help and not to harm.
He wants to embrace you with open arms.
Lord, help me to serve you not as a chore.
But give me Your heart, to show your love more.

What Do You Think?

Jesus said to love and forgive all your enemies. Does that mean even the Devil?

I don't know if this passage applies to the Devil or not. However, I pray that the Lord will help me to forgive people by giving me so much love for them that I can forgive even the Devil. I just pray for more of His Holy Spirit so that I can forgive anyone and anything. It is not good for people to keep hate for anyone, even the Devil, in their hearts.

I am not saying that we should become Devil worshippers and play with witchcraft. The Bible does say to resist the Devil and to hate evil. Just because you forgive someone does not mean you have to let them beat you up, rob you, and discourage your faith in Christ. Of course, the Devil will still have to answer for his sins.

I tried to forgive the Devil one night for what he did to me. It is weird. It is not like forgiving a person that you see on the earth. It took me a while to do it. When I finally forgave him, it felt like a giant weight lifting off me. I'm sure the Devil will still try to tempt me, call me names, persecute me, and declare all of my faults before God until the day I die.

I want to be able to forgive all of my enemies, even the Devil. I know that the Lord will help me to forgive my enemies and will heal the pain in my heart that they have caused.

There are many people reading this book that still want revenge on the Devil. If the Devil became powerless for one day, what would you do to him? Would you beat him with a bat? Would you get a gun and shoot him full of holes? Would you consider forgiving him?

I tell you, the best way to get revenge on the Devil is to forgive your brothers, sisters, parents, relatives, friends, and enemies. Forgive your boss for not acknowledging your accomplishments. Forgive your parents for trying to correct you the best way they could. Forgive your best friend who cheated behind your back with your boyfriend or girlfriend.

Through the love of Jesus, the power to forgive makes us more powerful then any demon in hell. If you hit Satan, he can hit you back. If you shoot him, he can shoot you back. However, if you forgive him, he cannot forgive back.

Forgiveness by the power of Jesus Christ gives us the ability to do something greater than Satan could ever dream of doing. Satan goes nuts trying to comprehend the logic of forgiveness. He wonders and ponders how someone can forgive the person who killed their son or daughter, the person who tells them they owe a thousand dollars in taxes, or the person who mistakes kindness for weakness and takes advantage over and over again.

Challenge

The Lord is always looking to give us more. The Devil is always looking to rob us and leave us with less.

The Devil wants us to live with unforgiveness towards other people. Demons go crazy over the concept of forgiveness because you can do something they cannot do, since they do not have the love of Jesus.

The best way to get revenge on the devil is to forgive others no matter who they are or what they have done. Take some time right now to ask the Lord to forgive all the people who have hurt you in the past. Don't do it for them. Give the Lord your all, as He did on the cross for us.

LESSON 37

Ethnocentric Pride

"Judge not, that ye be not judged.
For with what judgment ye judge, ye shall be judged: and with what
measure ye mete, it shall be measured to you again." (Matt. 7: 1-2)

Pride can come in many forms. There is the pride in which you think that you are better than everyone else. Then there is the pride where you don't want to ask anyone else for help. You are afraid that people will see you as weak if you go to anyone for help. Pride isolates people.

This next poem is about the pride of not asking anyone for help. When people have a problem, they need to ask the Lord for help. Sometimes the Lord will use others along our path to help us with our needs. All we have to do is ask.

Poem/Song

Mr. Smiley Face
I wake up Sunday Morning,
Before the sunrise dawning,
Before I go into my church,
And sit down on my perch.
Like a flood that has been contained inside.
A song comes from deep within my pride.

Chorus

No No No No. No. No. No. No.
Then my soul groans along side.
Oh Oh Oh Oh. Oh. Oh. Oh. Oh.
Suck in that gut. You better keep that smile.
You gotta keep the walk. Don't cramp your style.
Keep on goin; Just one more mile.
Just don't cry. It's only for a while.
One week I expected a promotion.
But instead I got a demotion.

My job was terminated.
And I was devastated.
I went to ask if people would pray.
But a voice restrained me and said to stay.
Like a flood that has been contained inside,
A song comes from deep within my pride.

Chorus

I decided to face this all alone.
So I went to get a loan.
Then I couldn't pay my debt.
I was out every dollar and cent.
I couldn't even afford to eat
With the pastor I was goin to meet.
Like a flood that has been contained inside,
A song comes from deep within my pride.

Chorus

So weeks continued by.
So in secret I would cry.
If I told the church my song,
I feared they'd think I did something wrong.
So because I fear what they ask.
To church I wear my smiley mask.
Like a flood that has been contained inside,
A song comes from deep within my pride.

Chorus

People kept asking me left and right.
They kept asking if I was all right.
I kept saying everything was okay,
Knowing I was lying every day.
All I said was "Hallelujah" and "Amen."
I kept anyone from coming in my head.
Like a flood that has been contained inside,
A song comes from deep within my pride.

Chorus

"Enough!!" I screamed in the church.
"I need help!" I yelled as I searched.
I was approached by all the guys and dames.
They helped me like in the book of James.
They didn't just pray, but act.
They helped to get my life intact.
Like a flood that has been contained inside,
A song comes from deep within my pride.
No No No No. No. No. No. No.
Then my soul growls along it's side.
Oh Oh Oh Oh. Oh. Oh. Oh. Oh.
Pride, you have to go. I got a real smile.
With me the Lord walks. I don't care about style.
I'm getting help. So I can go that mile.
I got Joy because I lost my problem pile.
Are people scared of being criticized?
Or if they tell their problems, would they be despised?
There is no longer that flood deep inside.
Because with the Lord and friends by my side
I trust that everything will be just fine.
This goes out to the churches in the land.
Always look to help and be a fan.

What Do You Think?

Pride has a lot of consequences. At the tower of Babel, because of our pride, the Lord confused the languages of everyone in the world. Man became divided.

It can be hard sometimes to love someone who speaks a different language. I wish so badly that I could communicate with everyone.

Once in a while, I have a Spanish-speaking client call at my job. I used to take Spanish in high school, but I still can't write or speak it fluently.

Sometimes, we see people from different countries and we complain about them because they don't know any English. We should not be impatient with these people, but should take the time to love them and get to know them.

We are lucky Jesus does not require us to speak Aramaic, as in Mel Gibson's film ***The Passion of the Christ.*** We are lucky we don't have to read Bibles in Hebrew and Greek, the original languages that were used to write the Old and New Testaments.

The Lord wants us to be a witness for Him to every people of every tongue, tribe, and nation. I would encourage everyone to study at least one other language so that we can spread the Gospel to these people.

Jesus died for people who speak English, Spanish, Greek, Italian, Chinese and every other language. Even if you can't really speak the language, you can still give someone a Bible or a Bible tract in their language and reach these people for Jesus.

Challenge

We need to show people that the Lord's love can overcome our pride and disobedience. His love goes beyond any tongue, tribe, and nation. Every group of people is precious in His sight.

Ask the Lord to fill you with love for people who are different from you.
Ask the Lord to help you to love them as He loves them.

Therefore are they before the throne of God, and serve Him day and night in His temple:

and He that sitteth on the throne shall dwell among them.

They shall hunger no more, neither thirst any more;

neither shall the sun light on them, nor any heat.

For the Lamb which is in the midst of the throne shall feed them, and shall lead them unto living fountains of water:

and God shall wipe away all tears from their eyes.

(Reve. 7: 15-17)

LESSON 38
A Blessed Life

"For thus saith the Lord of hosts; Yet once, it is a little while, and I will shake the heavens, and the earth, and the sea, and the dry land; And I will shake all nations, and the desire of all nations shall come: and I will fill this house with glory, saith the Lord of hosts." (Hagg. 2: 6-7)

I have experienced the Lord's love so greatly in my life. We all have stories to tell. As we press into the Lord and continue to live for Him, people are going to wonder why we are different. Why we do not worry when trials happen in our lives.

When people know that you are a follower of the Lord, people are watching you like a bug in a jar trying to figure you out. The best thing to do is to continue living for Christ and let His love shine through you.

This next poem was inspired by a good friend of mine who really loves the Lord. This friend once gave me a wooden piggy bank. She said she named the piggy bank Larry. I no longer have the pig but her love for the Lord is an everlasting inspiration to me.

Poem/Song

Larry the Pig

Narrator

Once upon a time, there was a pig named Larry,
Who always seemed to wear a smile and be merry.
Everyday, all over town
Larry never seemed to wear a frown.
One day, three little pigs looked at Larry boy
And decided to ask him why he had so much joy.
The first little pig, named Moe the Hog,
Looked at Larry like he was in the fog.

Moe the Hog

Larry, How come you are always happy and glad?
You don't have a lot of money, you should be sad.
I have lots of cash and money.
Why in the world are you so sunny?
This little piggy can go to the market.
You little Larry have to stay home.
This little piggy can have roast beef.
You little Larry have none.

Narrator

Larry rose up like he had wings.

Larry the Pig

It isn't all about material things.
Take it from me, it is no bluff,
There is more to joy than just having stuff.
The Lord is the provider of it all.
Joy cannot be bought in the mall.
It is the Lord who lives inside of me.
So with a snort and an oink, I go we we we.

Narrator

The second little pig, named Shemp the Boar,
Questioned Larry to find out more.

Shemp the Boar

Larry, you don't have prestige and fame,
No one really knows your name.
At my job, I am CEO.
There are a lot of people that I know.
Even with all your charity,
You just don't have popularity.
In this world, there are lots of dangers.
You got to know someone with all of these strangers.
When the Big Bad Wolf comes and you need help,
Who you gonna call when you whelp?

Narrator

Larry got up and started to speak,

Larry the Pig

I serve a strong God who isn't weak.
He is my security and my guide.
My God will protect me from the tide.
The Big Bad Wolf I don't have to fear.
In the name of Jesus, He is out of here.
I don't need to know a guy or dame.
All I have to know is Jesus' name.
It is the Lord who lives inside of me.
So with a snort and an oink, I go we we we.

Narrator

The third little pig, named Curly the Sow,
Questioned Larry to find out how.

Curly the Sow

Larry, why are you so happy in this world?
You are single. You don't have a girl.
I have a body that's out of sight.
I have a different pig to date every night.
How can you be happy so much?
When you don't get to feel that special touch.
Don't you ever feel alone?
With no girl calling you on the phone.

Narrator

Larry got up and cleared his throat.

Larry the Pig

I know that I am never alone.
Even though I don't have a clone.
I know the Lord, who is my friend.
He will always be there until the end.
All I need is the Lord's grace.
I don't need a pretty face.
Because I have Christ living in me,
So with a snort and an oink, I go we we we.

Narrator

So Larry went We We We all the way home.
Here is the moral of this poem.
Live always for the Lord and do what's right.
Because you never know when you are in someone's sight.
The Lord is calling us to this task.
So that we can share about Him when people ask.

Life Experience

The Lord has blessed me so much. I got my MBA in Accounting. Work is going well.

I have made a lot of friends over the years. I thank the Lord for every one of them.

I still ask the Lord for guidance concerning my relationship with Him, my job, where I live, whether I am to go for the CPA exam someday, a possible wife to settle down with, and other things. I know the Lord will show me when the time is right.

I hope my life experiences have helped you to see the need for the love of Jesus in your life. Only His love will overcome all obstacles in your life.

Challenge

Continue to study His word and prepare for when someone asks you about the Lord. I'm not saying to prepare a sermon. Let the Lord lead you. However, be ready to be used by Him.

Ask the Lord to give you divine appointments where you can share about Him.

LESSON 39

The Burning Building

"For there are three that bear record in heaven, the Father, the Word, and the Holy Ghost: and these three are one." (I John 5: 7)

Some churches do not preach the Trinity. Some will say that Jesus is just a person, a good teacher, or a great man. They may even admit that He is the Son of God, but they will not admit that Jesus is in fact God. Some churches even say that there is no Holy Spirit and no such thing as gifts of the Spirit. They say the gifts are not for today.

Our God consists of three persons. They are God the Father, God the Son, and the Holy Spirit. Each person of the Trinity serves a very important function.

This next poem explains the function of the Trinity. This poem starts off as a song and then continues as a poem. The words in bold are to be sung.

Poem/Song

The Three In Trinity
Holy Holy Holy
Lord God almighty,
God in three persons,
Blessed Trinity.

Chorus

Give a shout for victory!
Give it up for the Trinity!
Raise your hands in victory!
Give it up for the Trinity!
Come and join in the melody!
Give it up for the Trinity!
While we are in the victory
let me tell you about the Trinity
This is one God composed of three.

When you encounter adversity.
Look to the Lord for peace and tranquility.
Because in there you will find the victory.

Chorus

**One
Two
Three
Bop
Let me tell you about God the Pop.
He's the one who sits on top.
He created everything with just one stop.
When He speaks, Things start to bop.
Everyone give a shout and a hop.**

Chorus

**Count down
three
two
one.
Let me tell you about God the Son.
He died on the cross, so sin is done.
He rose from the grave and has won.
Jesus isn't just for pastors and nuns.
Come sing along and have some fun.**

Chorus

**Here's number three from coast to coast,
Let's give it up for the Holy Ghost.
He's not just sitting on a pedestal or post,
But here to comfort when you need Him most.
So with one shout give Him a toast.
of His love, It's okay to boast.**

Chorus:

**God in Three Persons,
Blessed Trinity**

What Do You Think?

There are many different models and situations people use to define the meaning of life. For instance, life can be like being trapped in a burning building with many floors.

When we start out in this world, we are destined for eternal punishment in hell due to our sinful nature. We are on a course that will lead to being burned to death with the building.

Luckily, the Lord provides each of us with a walkie talkie, an axe, and an oxygen tank with a mask. Unfortunately, not everyone accepts these gifts the Lord gives us.

Some people think they will avoid being burned by hiding in a closet or under the bed. This is a bad decision, because the firefighters will not know where they are. These people end up burning to death.

Some people think they can just hold their breath. Other people think they can get out without the walkie talkie, the axe, or the oxygen tank with the mask. These are people who try to use their own works and know how to get to heaven. Heaven is outside the building. Most of these people end up suffocating and burning to death.

The walkie talkie will help you get in contact with the firefighter outside the burning building. The firefighter outside the building represents God the Father. The firefighter is yelling instructions to you on how to get out of the building.

The walkie talkie represents prayer. Prayer is how we communicate with God and also how God communicates with us. Sometimes the signal is not clear on a walkie talkie. Sometimes it takes a couple of tries to hear what the other person is saying with all the static. This is why when you pray on an issue, you should persist until you are sure you understand what God is directing you to do.

Unfortunately, some people don't pick up the walkie talkie. They think they don't have to listen to the fireman and that they can find their own way out of the burning building. These are people who like to do things their own way instead of the Lord's way. Most of these people end up burning with the building.

The axe represents the Word of God. The axe is important because sometimes people will be trapped by the fire and have to chop their way through walls or floors to get out. In life, sometimes people encounter a wall or a floor. We are chopping away, but nothing seems to happen. The axe is working better than if you didn't have it and eventually the walls will come down.

Some people pick up the walkie talkie and the oxygen tank with the mask but leave the axe. Those who believe in the Father but not the Son do not truly believe in the Father.

Sometimes the firefighter on the walkie talkie will instruct us to knock some walls down to get out of the building. If you get trapped and don't have the axe, you will burn up and die.

The oxygen tank with the mask represents the Spirit of God. The Spirit of God gives us the power and strength we need to get outside the building. Sometimes the oxygen tank runs out of air. That is why it is important to refill it at a filling station. The filling station represents the church. When I say church, I am not talking about a physical structure. I am talking about a body of believers who love and seek the Lord with all their hearts, souls, and minds. As long as you keep going to church, you will have plenty of oxygen until you can get out of the building. If you stop going to church, you are not refilling your oxygen tank. Eventually, you will suffocate and die.

As one can see, the walkie talkie, the axe, and the oxygen tank with the mask are all essential in order to get out of the burning building and into heaven. They are all available to give us wisdom, direction, strength, power, removal of barriers sin puts in front of us, and the ability to chop through the times of trial.

Challenge

Will you accept God the Father, Jesus Christ, and the Holy Spirit into your heart so that you can avoid suffocating and burning to death? Eventually, a burning building will be destroyed. Will you still be inside the building or outside when it goes down?

Ask the Lord into your heart, soul, spirit, and life. Use the prayer in appendix A of the book if you need to. Spend some time giving thanks to all of the members of the Trinity.

LESSON 40

The Book of Nahum

"The Lord is good. A stronghold in times of trouble. He knoweth them
that put their trust in him." (Nahum 1:7)

There are a lot of complaints about the Bible. Some people claim that they do not have time in their busy schedule to read the Bible. While others say that the Bible is too difficult to understand. Because of this, a lot of people turn to other people or a formula for figuring the Lord out for their faith.

This next poem is about the book of Revelation. The devil will lie to people and say that this book is too difficult to understand. Others question how a loving God can go through with this plan. It all comes down to trusting in the Lord or believing the devil.

Poem/Song

Simple Revelation
As one continues to listen to the news
One can get so upset and confused
With all the chaos that has multiplied and grown.
In the book of Revelation, this is all shown.
This book was written by the Apostle John.
To the seven churches of which he is fond.
The churches are Ephesus, Pergamos, Smyrna, and Sardis,
Thyatira, Laodicia, & Philedelphia, the smartest.
John tells them what they do that's good and bad.
The Lord directs them to change, like a dad.
Some struggled with being too lukewarm.
Others to idols they did swarm.
Others did not do so well
Because they let people in possessed by Jezebel.
You may be shaking your head like you are confused,
But remember this song when it comes down to who you'll choose.

Chorus

Da Da Da Da
Da Da Da Da
Are you gonna be the Lord's squire?
And be dressed in white attire?
Are you gonna sing in the Lord's choir?
Holy Holy
to the One that's Higher.
Holy Holy
to the One that's Higher
Are you gonna go with Satan's desire?
And believe the big fat liar?
And thrown down when time expires
deep deep down
in the Lake of Fire?
deep deep down
in the Lake of Fire?
In chapters 4 & 5, there is quite a scene,
A throne and a rainbow in emerald green.
There are twenty four elders and four beasts unknown.
They are standing before God's throne.
A book with seven seals is in God's hand.
Only the Lamb, which is Jesus, is worthy to stand.
You may be shaking your head confused and in doubt.
But remember this song to help you out.

Chorus

The seals open one by one.
God's wrath has just begun.
There are horse riders colored in white, red, black, and pale,
To kill the fourth part of the Earth they will set sail.
Before the throne are martyred saints.
They are wearing white robes that God taints.
The sun turns black and the moon turns red.
Oh, the wicked of the Earth start to dread.
Four angels are then holding back the wind.
God's seal is in those that sexually have not sinned.
These are 144,000 Jewish virgin men
Who reach the lost like a mother hen.
Now the Devil is very diabolic.
He will tell you this is all symbolic.
But are you gonna believe the Lord who should be adored?
Remember this song when you pick a side to board.

Chorus

The seventh seal is released.
The noise in Heaven just suddenly ceased.
Seven angels with trumpets came around.
They stood together and started to sound.
A third of the plants and water were destroyed,
and a third of the heavens became a dark void.
When angel five began to play
The locusts began to have a field day.
The people were in so much pain,
Then angel six sounded just the same,
And a third of the people were all slain.
And the people left still refused to call on Jesus' name.
Ask yourself, whose name are you gonna call?
Here's a song to summarize it all.

Chorus

In chapter 10, we see an angel with a book.
He had the face of the sun and feet hot enough to cook.
Then in Heaven, it quaked and thundered.
John could not write down what was uttered.
John was told to take the book and eat.
In the belly it was bitter, in the mouth it was sweet.
In chapter 11, we see two witnesses as olive trees.
They will shake the world to its knees.
They stop the rain and from their mouths shoots fire.
These two the beast does not desire.
For three and a half days, they are left for dead.
But they will rise up and cause the world dread.
There will be earthquakes and woes
As the seventh angel blows.
The world is now ruled by the Lord.
As you hear this song, choose the side you're gonna board.

Chorus

Next we see in the heavens a woman with a child to be born.
We see a dragon with seven heads and ten horns to be a thorn.
There's a war between the angels and the Dragon's demons,
But the Lamb casts those demons down screamin.

This war still continues to this day.
Now we look out towards the sea and the bay.
We see the beast and false prophet come up from the deep.
And the world will follow them like gullible sheep.
But with the saints they will light a spark
Because the saints won't accept the Antichrist's mark.
You may ask "Is this beast a president, king, or pope?"
Don't ponder this, look to the Lord for hope.
You may wonder if the mark is a sign or a chip,
But you should consider the song in this next clip.

Chorus

We next see the 144,000 as a group on the mountaintop,
Singing their secret song of rock and pop.
Then we see angels flying overhead,
Saying "Worship the Lord or you will be dead."
The one who was conceived in a virgin birth
Is getting ready to harvest the Earth.
Seven angels come out with vials with the last plagues.
They are wearing golden girdles and white linen, not rags.
As those vials the angels hold start to pour,
The people with the beast's mark start to get sore.
Water turns to blood. people are scorched by the sun.
The beast and his people are not having fun.
The seventh vial is poured, it begins to hail,
But the beast and his people in Armageddon will fail.
Are you gonna be the head or the tail?
Here is the chorus again to unveil.

Chorus

Next, we see a woman dressed in purple and scarlet.
She will seduce the kings of the land as a harlot.
The woman represents Babylon, a city.
For the saints there just is no pity.
But this city is gonna go down.
And the people of the world will weep all around.
And the people of God will rejoice.
Because the city killed them for their choice.
Don't look so puzzled and confused.
Here's a song to help you choose.

Chorus

In chapter 19, we see the next course,
A rider mounted on a white horse,
The Lord of Lords and the King of Kings.
An angel calls each bird that sings.
To eat the flesh of those of worldly attire.
The beast, false prophet, and their agents of evil desire
Are cast deep deep down in the lake of fire.
And the Devil that big fat liar.
Will be bound a millennium in a pit,
While the saints of God as kings and queens will sit.
After the millennium, the Devil will be let out,
To find those who he can cause to doubt,
And lead them against God and His holy city.
But they will be judged with the Devil and that's a pity.
The Devil will be judged by the Lord and all His choir,
And will be thrown deep deep down in the Lake of Fire.
Now ask yourself what you desire.
I hope this song will cause you to inspire.

Chorus

There'll be a new heaven and earth in the end.
There is a New Jerusalem for our den.
God will wipe away every tear.
No more hunger, anger, sorrow, or fear.
The city will have twelve gates.
The Lamb and the bride become the best of mates.
There will be no sun or moon that will shine,
Because the Lord's glory will do just fine.
And a river of life runs from God's throne,
All of you saints, go make this known.
The Lord is coming very soon.
Proclaim to the nations this revelation tune.

Chorus
Da Da Da Da
Da Da Da Da

What Do You Think?

A lot of people don't realize that the book of Nahum is in the Bible. A lot of people would say that they never heard their pastors say anything from the book of Nahum or any of the other lesser known books of the Bible.

Why is it that people put their trust in a person who stands on a pulpit on Sunday mornings for their salvation? Do you tell someone to get a paper, read it, and tell you what happens in the newspaper? No, you go and buy the newspaper *yourself* and read it *yourself*. Why are people so quick to believe what is in the newspaper but doubt the words in the Bible? How much more important is your salvation than anything else.

The problem with not reading the Bible is that when someone talks to us about the Lord, we need to know if it is truly someone sent by the Lord or an agent of the Devil trying to lead us astray.

Even the Devil used scripture when he was trying to tempt Jesus out in the wilderness. Jesus was able to overcome these temptations because He constantly studied the scriptures and asked His Father for strength and wisdom.

Jesus came to this world not only to die for our sins. He came also to be an example of how we can live for the Lord. We need to ask the Lord to reveal the scriptures to us.

Challenge

It is good to go to church, but also read His word for yourself. If you don't understand a passage, keep reading it and inquire of God to help you understand the meaning of the passage.

Take some time to read the Bible. Pick a book of the Bible, such as the book of Nahum or the book of Revelation, that you are not too familiar with or that seems difficult to understand and read it. As you read, ask the Lord to reveal to you what is being said in these books. Remember that every one of His words is precious.

LESSON 41
God Send Me

"Wherefore we receiving a kingdom which cannot be moved, let us have grace, whereby we may serve God acceptably with reverence and godly fear:"
(Hebr. 12:28)

No man can serve two masters; either He will love the one or hate the other, or He will submit to the one and loathe the other. We cannot have one foot in the Lord's kingdom and one foot in the world.

A lot of people believe that when you are a Christian you are in bondage to all these rules. But when we become Christians, we are set free from sin. Sin is addicting and true bondage.

This next poem shows how the story of Pinnochio compares to our walk with the Lord. We all have to make a choice. Are we going to choose the Lord as our master or the Devil?

Poem/Song

Pinnochio
I am His Pinnochio,
He is my Geppetto.
Some people look at me as God's puppet,
Like I'm Kermit the Frog or a Muppet.
They ask me "How can you let God pull your strings?"
You have to go to church and you can't do lots of things.
You can't drink. You can't lie. You have to be nice.
You can't lust for men and women who entice.
With him pulling your strings, how can you live.
When you can't partake in fun things this world has to give?
My reply is that I am His Pinnochio.
He is my Geppetto.
I may not do things that are wicked.
But I need Jesus like Jiminy Cricket.
Here is a statement that may sting.
But we are all puppets on a string.
However we have a right to choose
who controls all our moves.
Are we going to be led by the Devil or the Lord?

Who is going to control this wooden board?
I am His Pinnochio.
He is my Geppetto.
When I open up my mouth to speak,
I want only the Lord's words to leak.
I want the Lord's energy and pep.
I want the Lord to move my every step.
Better His puppet than a donkey or an ass.
The thought of Satan controlling me, I think I'll pass.
I don't want to be lead to destruction or jail.
Or end up like Jonah in the belly of the whale.
I am His Pinnochio.
He is my Geppetto.
I want to be led by His truth, love, and joy,
That makes everyone feel like a real girl or boy.
The Lord will use me to lead others like a pastor.
It is better that Jesus Christ is your Master.
With Jesus you will be truly set free,
So that you honestly say, "There ain't no strings on me."

What Do You Think?

Why does everything seem to happen all at once? It is hard sometimes to drop what you are doing to do something the Lord tells you to do.

Some people just stand in the church and sing to the Lord "God send me," yet when the Lord wants to send them, they are quick to rationalize, "Lord surely not me and not to do that."

We must do what the Lord wants us to do in order to advance his kingdom. We must proclaim Him, because Jesus is proclaiming to God the Father that He loves us despite all the faults of our sinful nature.

We must go out into the world to reach the lost because He came into the world to save us.

Challenge

We all have to make a choice. Are we going to serve the Lord or are we going to serve the Devil?

I would encourage you to rent or buy the movie Pinnochio and watch it not as a Disney movie but as a Holy Spirit-filled movie.

If you cannot watch the movie, think to yourself about movies or stories that you have seen or heard that could reflect our walk with the Lord.

Then ask the Lord to show you what He wants you to do.

LESSON 42

Grand Finale

"I am Alpha and Omega, the beginning and the ending, saith the Lord, which is, and which was, and which is to come, the Almighty." (Reve. 1:8)
And they all lived happily ever after.

I don't like this ending very well. Nobody ever had any more problems. No one still had things they had to accomplish. I guess Cinderella and Prince Charming never had any fights once they were married. Did the two little pigs build brick houses like the third little pig after their encounter with the wolf, or did they continue to be just as lazy and live in straw and stick houses like nothing ever happened?

I was praying for wisdom on how to end this book. I started thinking about how the books in the Bible ended.

In the next section, I have made a list of the last verse of every book in the Bible from Genesis to Revelation.

Old Testament

"So Joseph died, being an hundred and ten years old: and they embalmed him, and he was put in a coffin in Egypt" (Gen. 50:26)
"For the cloud of the Lord was upon the tabernacle by day, and fire was on it by night, in the sight of all the house of Israel, throughout all their journeys." (Exo. 40:38)
"These are the commandments, which the Lord commanded Moses for the children of Israel in Mount Sinai." (Lev. 27:34)
"These are the commandments and the judgments, which the Lord commanded by the hand of Moses unto the children of Israel in the plains of Moab by Jordan near Jericho." (Num. 36:13)
"And in all that mighty hand and in all the great terror which Moses showed in the sight of all Israel." (Deut. 34:12)
"And Eleazar the son of Aaron died; and they buried him in a hill that pertained to Phinehas his son, which was given him in Mount Ephraim." (Josh. 24:33)

"In those days there was no king in Israel: every man did that which was right in his own eyes." (Judg. 21:25)

"And Obed begat Jesse, and Jesse begat David." (Ruth 4:22)

"And they took their bones, and buried them under a tree at Jabesh, and fasted seven days." (I Sam. 31: 13)

"And David built there an altar unto the Lord, and offered burnt offerings and peace offerings. So the Lord was entreated for the land, and the plague was stayed from Israel" (2 Sam. 24:25)

"For he served Baal, and worshipped him, and provoked to anger the Lord God of Israel, according to all that his father had done." (I Kings 22:53)

"And his allowance was a continual allowance given him of the king, a daily rate for every day, all the days of his life." (2 Kings 25:30)

"With all his reign and his might, and the times that went over him, and over Israel, and over all the kingdoms of the countries." (I Chron. 29:30)

"Thus saith Cyrus king of Persia, All the kingdoms of the Earth hath the Lord God of heaven given me; and he hath charged me to build him an house in Jerusalem, which is in Judah. Who is there among you of all his people? The Lord his God be with him, and let him go up." (2 Chron. 36: 23)

"All these had taken strange wives: and some of them had wives by whom they had children." (Ezra 10:44)

"And for the wood offering, at times appointed, and for the firstfruits. Remember me, O my God, for good." (Nehe. 13:31)

"For Mordecai the Jew was next unto King Ahasuerus, and great among the Jews, and accepted of the multitude of his brethren, seeking the wealth of his people, and speaking peace to all his seed." (Esth. 10:3) "So Job died, being old and full of days." (Job 42: 17)

"Let every thing that hath breath praise the Lord. Praise ye the Lord." (Psal. 150:6)

"Give her of the fruit of her hands; and let her own works praise her in the gates." (Prov. 31: 31)

"For God shall bring every work into judgment, with every secret thing, whether it be good, or whether it be evil." (Eccl. 12: 14)

"Make haste, my beloved, and be thou like to a roe or to a young hart upon the mountains of spices." (Song. 8: 14)

"And they shall go forth, and look upon the carcasses of the men that have transgressed against me: for their worm shall not die, neither shall their fire be quenched; and they shall be an abhorring unto all flesh." (Isai. 66: 24)

"And for his diet, there was a continual diet given him of the King of Babylon, every day a portion until the day of his death, all the days of his life." (Jere. 52: 34)

"But thou hast utterly rejected us; thou art very wroth against us." (Lam. 5: 22)

"It was round about eighteen thousand measures: and the name of the city from that day shall be, The Lord is there." (Ezek. 48: 35)

"But go thou thy way till the end be: for thou shalt rest, and stand in thy lot at the end of the days." (Dan. 12: 13)

"Who is wise, and he shall understand these things? Prudent, and he shall know them? For the ways of the Lord are right, and the just shall walk in them: but the transgressors shall fall therein." (Hosea 14: 9)

"For I will cleanse their blood that I have not cleansed: for the Lord dwelleth in Zion." (Joel 3: 21)

"And I will plant them upon their land, and they shall no more be pulled up out of their land which I have given them, saith the Lord thy God." (Amos 9:15)

"And saviors shall come up on Mount Zion to judge the Mount of Esau; and the kingdom shall be the Lord's." (Obad. 1: 21)

"And should not I spare Ninevah, that great city, wherein are more than six score thousand persons that cannot discern between their right hand and their left hand; and also much cattle?" (Jonah 4: 11)

"Thou wilt perform the truth to Jacob, and the mercy to Abraham, which thou hast sworn unto our fathers from the days of old." (Micah 7:20)

"There is no healing of thy bruise; thy wound is grievous: all that hear the bruit of thee shall clap the hands over thee: for upon whom hath not thy wickedness passed continually?" (Nahum 3: 19)

"The Lord God is my strength, and he will make my feet like hinds' feet, and he will make me to walk upon mine high places. To the chief singer on my stringed instruments." (Haba. 3: 19)

"At that time will I bring you again, even in the time that I gather you: for I will make you a name and a praise among all people of the Earth, when I turn back you captivity before your eyes, saith the Lord." (Zeph. 3: 20)

"In that day, saith the Lord of hosts, will I take thee, O Zerrubbabel, my servant, the son of Shealtiel, saith the Lord, and will make thee as a signet: for I have chosen thee, saith the Lord of hosts." (Hagg. 2: 23)

"Yea, every pot in Jerusalem and in Judah shall be holiness unto the Lord of hosts: and all they that sacrifice shall come and take of them, and seethe therein: and in that day there shall be no more the Canaanite in the house of the Lord of hosts." (Zech. 14: 21)

"And he shall turn the heart of the fathers to the children, and the heart of the children to their fathers, lest I come and smite the Earth with a curse." (Mala. 4: 6)

New Testament

"Teaching them to observe all things whatsoever I have commanded you: and, lo, I am with you always, even unto the end of the world. Amen." (Matt. 28:20)

"And they went forth, and preached every where, the Lord working with them, and confirming the word with signs following. Amen." (Mark 16:20)

"And were continually in the temple, praising and blessing God. Amen." (Luke 24:53)

"And there are also many other things which Jesus did, the which, if they should be written every one, I suppose that even the world itself could not contain the books that should be written. Amen." (John 21:25)

"Preaching the kingdom of God, and teaching those things which concern the Lord Jesus Christ, with all confidence, no man forbidding him." (Acts 28:31)

"To God only wise, be glory through Jesus Christ for ever. Amen." (Roma. 16:27)

"My love be with you all in Christ Jesus. Amen." (I Cori. 16: 24)

"The grace of the Lord Jesus Christ, and the love of God, and the communion of the Holy Ghost, be with you all. Amen." (2 Cori. 13:14)

"Brethren, the grace of our Lord Jesus Christ be with your spirit. Amen." (Gala. 6:18)

"Grace be with all them that love our Lord Jesus Christ in sincerity. Amen." (Ephe. 6:24)

"The grace of our Lord Jesus Christ be with you all. Amen." (Phil. 4:23)

"The salutation by the hand of me Paul. Remember my bonds, Grace be with you. Amen." (Colo. 4:18)

"The grace of our Lord Jesus Christ be with you. Amen." (I Thes. 5: 28)

"The grace of our Lord Jesus Christ be with you all. Amen." (2 Thes. 3:18)

"Which some professing have erred concerning the faith. Grace be with thee. Amen." (I Timo. 6:21)

"The Lord Jesus Christ be with thy spirit. Grace be with you. Amen." (2 Timo. 4:22)

"All that are with me salute thee. Greet them that love us in the faith. Grace be with you all. Amen." (Titus 3:15)

"The grace of our Lord Jesus Christ be with your spirit. Amen." (Phil. 1: 25)

"Grace be with you all. Amen." (Hebr. 13:25)

"Let him know, that he which converteth the sinner from the error of his way shall save a soul from death, and shall hide a multitude of sins." (James 5:20)

"Greet ye one another with a kiss of charity. Peace be with you all that are in Christ Jesus. Amen." (I Pet. 5:14)

"But grow in grace, and in the knowledge of our Lord and Savior Jesus Christ. To him be glory both now and for ever. Amen." (2 Pet. 3:18)

"Little children, keep yourselves from idols. Amen." (I John 5:21)

"The children of thy elect sister greet thee. Amen." (2 John 1:13)
"But I trust that I shall shortly see thee, and we shall speak face to face.
Peace be to thee. Our friends salute thee. Greet the friends by name."
(3 John 1:14)
"To the only wise God our Savior, be glory and majesty, dominion and
power, both now and ever. Amen." (Jude 1:25)
"The grace of our Lord Jesus Christ be with you all. Amen." (Reve. 22:21)

What Do You Think?

How do you want your life to end? Do you want your life to end like the book of Mark and see His signs and wonders? Do you want it to end like the book of First Kings by continuing to sin and provoke the Lord to anger? Do you think it is a happy ending if your story ends like the book of Genesis, where you just live a good life here, get buried in the ground, and that's it? What about the rest of eternity?

You may have had a bad start, and what you are going through right now is unbearable. Don't use this as an excuse to drop out of the race and give up. Keep moving forward no matter how hard life gets.

God never said things would be easy. Love is not easy. It takes a lot of work. Look at what Jesus did to show His love for us in dying on the cross.

Challenge

Confess your sins to the Lord. Accept Him into your heart and soul. A prayer has been provided in Appendix A to show you how to accept the Lord into your life and to experience the love He has for you.

After you say this prayer, continue to pray to the Lord daily for direction. Read and study His Word, the Bible. I suggest you begin with the Gospel of John and then Matthew, Mark, and Luke. See what Jesus said and did. Get to know Jesus. Pray and ask the Lord to lead you and guide you each and every day.

Don't make this the end of the story. Make this the beginning.

Appendix A

Prayer to Accept the Lord Into Your Life

Father God
I am a sinner. Please forgive my sin. I believe Jesus Christ, Your Son, died
on the cross for my sins and rose again on the third day.
Lord Jesus, come into my heart and life. Be my personal
Savior and Lord. I choose to be a new creature in You.
Show me the things that are not of You which keep me from experiencing
Your love for me.
I dedicate my life to You. It is no longer I who live, but Christ who lives
within me. Not just for today, but every day.
Help me to listen for Your voice and keep Your love deep within my heart.
I am now Your child. The Devil has no control over me. Guide me into
Your will and Your purpose for my life.
Help me to show others the love You have for them. True love is meant to
be shared. Please continue to reveal Your love with me.
In Jesus' Name.
Amen.

Appendix B

Poem Finder

Poem/Song	Lesson # Where Poem is Found
A Question to Ponder Sometimes	21
Bad Day	3
Buzy Body Bees	11
Carry Me	20
Catfood	26
Charcoal	25
Christmas Debate	12
Countdown	16
Distraction	34
Go Ye Into All the World	28
God's Heart	36
Heart of a Giant	19
How Much	35
Insane about the Rain	32
It's Not Just About the Turkey	2
Jesus Wept	27
Job's Blue Song	24
Keep Quiet	9
Larry the Pig	38
Your Light Shine Before Men	31
Mr. Smiley Face	37
Our God is Out of the Box	1
Payback	18
Perfect Gifts	10
Pinnochio	41

Appendix C

Additional Poem/Songs

The Lord has many titles. One is the Greater Healer. The Lord created our bodies. This means that the Lord knows exactly what our bodies need in order to function at their best. He is the Great Physician.

However, sometimes we limit the Lord in a certain area of our lives. Some of us, trust the Lord as our protector but take the word of a doctor over the Lord's word. Others trust Him with their lives and time but not with their finances.

This next poem was written to show the people of God that we need to trust Him enough to believe that He can heal us of anything and fix all of our situations.

Poem/Song

The Doctor
I wake up to a new day.
I ask for victory as I pray.
However with daily aches and pain,
I call on just one name.
All the earthly doctors and man
Have done for me all that they can.
But there is still one more source
That can heal my wounds and change my course.
There is a God who reigns on high,
Who can heal the pain that makes me cry.
He has more wisdom than a PhD.
Through Him we will achieve the victory.
With all of His glory and power,
He can give a Holy Spirit shower.
He can heal and make you whole,
sing to your body and your soul.

Chorus
Line up. Line up.
In Jesus' name line up.
Every sickness must bow.

Every curse is broken now.
My wounds will heal.
His blood has sealed the deal.
Line up. Line up. Line up.
In Jesus' name.
Line up. Line up. Line up.
He will take away the fear and doubt.
And He will cast all the junk on out.
But, before He can move in
Confess to Him your sin.
Don't explain away your sin and hide.
Ask Him to forgive you for your pride.
Lord, open all the ears and eyes,
And cast out all the doubt and lies.
Lord, we ask that you come around,
And knock us to the ground.
Your Word is more than a fable.
So, I go on the operating table.
You can heal and make me whole.
I sing now to my body and my soul.

Chorus

I confess that His Word is true.
His love can take away what's blue.
I don't want to just survive but live.
Show me, Lord, who I'm to forgive.
Unforgiveness, you have to leave.
The junk please prune away and cleave.
The Devil can no longer rob
When you let Him do His job.
My soul, Lord, please help restore,
And Holy Spirit, just fill me more.
Lord knock my body onto the ground.
Oh, your love and glory will astound.
He can heal and make you whole.
Sing to your body and your soul.

Chorus
When you give Him all the junk and sin.
Now His work He can begin.
We command the body to line up right,
In Jesus' name bring it to sight.

The Devil and his demons must flee.
Disease and illness, you cannot be.
He can give new life to dry bones.
He can heal your finances and reduce your loans.
Any injury from a fall or a crash.
We leave behind us in the trash.
Anything men have said or done.
Can be healed through Jesus Christ the Son.
The lame will walk,
And the dumb will talk.
He can restore my nerves and spine,
And make everything just fine.
He can heal and make you whole.
Sing to your body and your soul.

Chorus

With all the death and sickness lurking.
Praise the Lord that He is always working.
He will help you with any wounds you detect.
The best part is there is no side effect.
We cancel all the effects from prescriptions and pills.
Ask the Lord to deliver you from all of life's spills.
Praise Him for all that He has done in your life.
Don't forget Him. Love Him as a husband and wife.
As long as you seek Him, He will continue to heal.
Your wounds and your sickness will have to kneel.
To the Lord remember to tithe and bow,
And He will leave you saying, "Wow."
He can heal and make you whole.
Sing to your body and your soul.

Chorus

And the blind will see.
Turn to Him and believe.
Line up. Line up. Line up.
In Jesus name.
Line up. Line up. Line up.
Line up in Jesus' name.

Appendix C

Additional Poem/Songs

People claim that we have freedom of speech in this nation. However, it seems to be just the freedom to speak what is evil and wicked. What about the freedom to talk about the Lord and to speak about things that are good?

In this nation, there are a lot of places where if you talk about the Lord, you are silenced. People are also scared to say something nice to other people for fear of rejection.

This next poem was written to get people to fight for the freedom to not just speak about the bad things in life but to speak words of encouragement and to speak about the Lord.

Poem/Song

Censored
There are many bad words
That are spoken throughout our herds.
There is the F word that rhymes with truck.
Oh, for every time I've heard it if I could just get a buck.
There are many more spoken in songs and in rap.
These are all words that all mean crap.
When speaking about Beep, we have to watch what we say.
In school and at work, we are made to feel ashamed to pray.
People can say any negative thing.
But for Beep I cannot sing.

Chorus

Ba Ba Beep
Ba Ba Beep
Why is it for Him I cannot speak?
Ba Ba Beep
Ba Ba Beep
Freedom of speech went up the creek.

I can speak all the bad things if I could.
But I also want the freedom to speak good.
Ba Ba Beep Ba Ba Beep
Ba Ba Ba Ba Ba Ba Beep
There are so many words designed to hurt.
All these evil words people can freely blurt.
I gotta shake my head the way people just nod,
Except when you mention Beep the Son of God
The word god you can freely speak, say, or sing,
Because it could mean anyone or anything.
Your god could be Muhammad, Buddha, Zeus, or an idea,
But if you mean Beep, the Devil don't want anyone to hear.
People can say any negative thing.
But for Beep I cannot sing.

Chorus

How come it is so hard to say something nice
But easy to say words that can hurt and slice?
Just to say a phrase wishing happy cheer,
We are told not to speak about Beep or "Get outta here."
Try to talk about the one who died for sin on the cross.
How many can talk about Beep at work in front of your boss?
Talk about Beep in the parks and on the street.
Are you told to tune down the beat?
At the end of the year, people are told to say.
Instead of Beep Beep, say Happy Holiday.
People can say any negative thing.
But for Beep I cannot sing.

Chorus

Why do people look for the faults,
And speak bad things with no halts?
Why can't we look at what's good,
And talk about the strengths, as we should?
Sticks and stones may break my bones,
But words can hurt spoken on streets and phones.
People can walk around on TV in their underwear,
But if you speak about Beep you get a rotten stare.
Speak about positive things, people wonder why.
It is like a crime just to say "Hi."
People can say any negative thing,
But for Beep I cannot sing.

Chorus

There has to be a way I can preach and proclaim.
There has got to be a way I can say Beep's name.
Why can't I have the freedom to talk about Him and heaven.
Boy, we can't even mention Him during 9/11.
There has to be a way to promote the good news.
To speak His name I want to do if I so choose.
We have to speak about Him to keep people from going to hell.
But maybe with some thinking, I can use my ability to spell.
We have to proclaim His name because we care,
Even if it means being kicked off the air.

JESUS
He loves you and He's the very best.
JESUS
His love reaches from the east to the west.
JESUS
He's the one who can show you what's true.
JESUS
Loves you.
Ba Ba Beep.

We are now experiencing technical difficulties. Please stand by.